# POETRY & POLITICS

THE WILES LECTURES
GIVEN AT THE QUEEN'S UNIVERSITY
BELFAST 1965

# POETRY & POLITICS
## 1900-1960

BY

## C.M.BOWRA

*Warden of Wadham College, Oxford*

CAMBRIDGE
AT THE UNIVERSITY PRESS
1966

PUBLISHED BY

THE SYNDICS OF THE CAMBRIDGE UNIVERSITY PRESS

Bentley House, 200 Euston Road, London, N.W. 1
American Branch: 32 East 57th Street, New York, N.Y. 10022
West Africa Office: P.M.B. 5181, Ibadan, Nigeria

©

CAMBRIDGE UNIVERSITY PRESS

**1966**

*Printed in Great Britain at the University Printing House, Cambridge*
*(Brooke Crutchley, University Printer)*

LIBRARY OF CONGRESS CATALOGUE
CARD NUMBER: 66–17056

# CONTENTS

# PREFACE

This book contains four lectures which I had the honour of delivering in May 1965 in the Queen's University, Belfast on the invitation of the Wiles Foundation. The text as printed is rather longer than what I actually delivered, when each lecture had to be confined to an hour, but I have made no substantial alterations. I have added a few notes, mainly to give references to the texts from which my quotations are drawn but partly to quote more fully passages to which I have done no more than refer to in the lectures.

My warmest thanks are due to the Wiles Foundation and to all those who helped to make my visit to Belfast agreeable, particularly to Dr Michael Grant, Vice-Chancellor of the Queen's University, and to Mrs Grant for their charming hospitality; to Mrs Austin Boyd and to Professor Michael Roberts for many kindnesses. Though I learned much in the discussions which took place after each lecture, I have not ventured to claim as my own any suggestions made in them.

I am also grateful to the staff of the Cambridge University Press for the care which they have taken with the printing of the book, and to Mr E. T. Webb for making the Index.

C. M. B.

*Oxford*
*January 1966*

# ACKNOWLEDGEMENTS

I am grateful to the following for permission to reproduce material in the Lectures: to the Oxford University Press for the *Poems of Gerald Manley Hopkins*; to Macmillan & Co. Ltd., The Macmillan Company and the Trustees of the Hardy Estate for the *Collected Poems* of Thomas Hardy; to the author and New Directions, Inc. for Ezra Pound's *Selected Poems*; to Mrs W. B. Yeats, Macmillan & Co. Ltd. and the Macmillan Company for W. B. Yeats's *Collected Poems*; to the author and Oxford University Press for David Gascoyne's *Poems, 1937–42*; to the Edith Sitwell Estate for Edith Sitwell's *Collected Poems*; to Faber & Faber Ltd. and Harcourt, Brace and World, Inc. for T. S. Eliot's *Collected Poems, 1909–62*; to Routledge & Kegan Paul Ltd. for the *Collected Poems of Sidney Keyes*; to the Literary Executors of the Dylan Thomas Estate, J. M. Dent & Sons Ltd. and New Directions, Inc. for Dylan Thomas's *Collected Poems, 1934–52*; to the John Day Co. Inc. for Peter H. Lee's *Anthology of Korean Poetry*; to the author and Frederick A. Praeger, Inc. for S. Yesenin-Volpin's *A Leaf of Spring*; to The Clarendon Press for B. W. Andrzejewski and I. M. Lewis's *Somali Poetry*; to the author, Rex Warner, the Bodley Head Ltd. and Little, Brown & Co. for Mr Warner's translation of George Seferis's *Poems*; and to the author, Weidenfeld & Nicolson Ltd. and the World Publishing Company for George Reavey's *The Bed-bug and Selected Poetry by Vladimir Mayakovsky*.

C. M. B.

## CHAPTER I

# THE CHANGE OF ATTITUDE

Many people dislike the notion that poetry can have any connection with politics and think that, even if we extend politics to cover a whole range of public events, it stands in an awkward relation to poetry, that its incursions are usually unsuccessful and often deplorable, and that its influence defiles an otherwise pure art. Yet public themes have for centuries been common in many parts of the world and the conscious avoidance of them is more often the exception than the rule. They were never far from the minds of the Greeks, who might sometimes disguise them in myth and symbol but were certainly not shy of them and admired such poets as Simonides and Aeschylus who wrote of them on a generous scale. Virgil and Horace owe to their political disquisitions at least half their renown, to say nothing of their canonisation in the curricula of British schools. In the *Divine Comedy* politics is quite as fundamental as theology and certainly more dramatic, and Dante shows his taste for it when he places one pope, Celestine V, 'who made the great refusal', in Limbo,[1] and another, Boniface VIII, in Hell.[2] Poets of the Romantic age found in public actions both at home and abroad rich opportunities for the denunciation of old systems and the imaginative delineation of new. In our own century, with its crowded record of wars international and civil, of social revolutions and awakening continents, of vigorous and often vicious reappraisals of what man owes to himself, poets can hardly be expected to keep clear of politics in the general sense of contemporary public affairs. Some have tried to do so and failed; others have not even tried. If much political verse is not worth the paper on which it is written, that is after all true of most verse on most subjects at most periods and does not discredit the small amount of authentic poetry which defies the corrosion of time. There is in principle a case to treat political poetry seriously and to attempt some consideration of what it has done in our own century.

The essence of this poetry is that it deals with events which concern a large number of people and can be grasped not as immediate, personal experience but as matters known largely from hearsay and presented in simplified and often abstract forms. It is thus the antithesis of all poetry which deals with the special, individual activity of the self and tries to present this as specially and as individually as it can. The poet who deals with public themes may himself be affected, even deeply, by contemporary events at some point in his own being, but to see them in their breadth and depth he must rely largely on what he hears from other men and from mass instruments of communication. From the start his impulse to write about them is different from any impulse to write about his own affairs. It may be just as strong and just as compelling, but it is not of the same kind. He has to give his own version of something which millions of others may share with him, and however individual he may wish to be, he cannot avoid relying to a large extent on much that he knows only from second-hand. Fundamentally, this may not matter; for after all what else did Shakespeare do? But the political poet does not construct an imaginary past; he attempts to grasp and interpret a vast present. Between him and his subject there is a gap which he can never completely cross, and all his attempts to make events part of himself must be to some extent hampered by recalcitrant elements in them, which he does not understand or cannot assimilate or finds irrelevant to his creative task. In such poetry selection, which is indispensable to all art, has to be made from an unusually large field of possibilities and guided by an exacting sense of what really matters and what does not. On one side he may try to include too much and lose himself in issues where he is not imaginatively at home; on the other side he may see some huge event merely from a private angle which need not mean much to others. Political poetry oscillates between these extremes, and its history in our own time has been largely of attempts to make the best of one or the other of them or to see what compromises can be made between them.

Modern achievement in political and public poetry stands out more clearly if we set it against what was written in the latter half of the nineteenth century. Though this period lacked upheavals comparable in scale to our own, it had enough to give a marked direction to its feelings on general issues. Its poetry is often effective and sometimes distinguished, but it has notable limitations. Despite its eloquence and its zest it seems unable to go as far as it might even with those themes with which it is most concerned. This is perhaps characteristic of the nineteenth century in more than one activity and reflects a society which, despite its lofty aims and its busy conscience, suffered from a certain blindness just because it was secure and prevented by its very security from questioning too closely the basis of its existence. Just as Dickens will pass penetrating criticisms on society and then pull up suddenly and not pursue them to their conclusion, so even the best poets will attack an important theme in an outspoken and original manner only to reveal that ultimately their thoughts about it are commonplace. We must not look to them for surprising illuminations. Such were not their aim, and perhaps they were incapable of them. What they excelled at was a handsome treatment, in their own high language, of themes which were familiar to everyone and on which there was a more or less established and accepted attitude. Poets spoke consciously and conscientiously for a whole people or a whole class. What they said was marked and quoted and might even influence public opinion. If, in speaking as they did, they repressed something that was most personal in themselves, at least they represented a large mass of sentiment to which they gave shape and style. They usually wrote at some distance from their actual themes and even from their own private feelings, and, since most public issues seldom affected their lives at all seriously, they saw them as abstract causes which called for general principles and generous emotions. They might have private reservations about them, but

1-2

they thought that these were irrelevant to their public duty. No doubt they believed what they said, but it may not have been all that they believed. What counted with them was that they were public figures who spoke on public matters, and that is why their utterances were shaped by concessions and compromises between them and their readers.

The strength of this poetry comes from the poet's conviction that he speaks for a mass of people who share his outlook and his interests. He addresses a large audience in the knowledge that many already agree with him on his main tenets and in the hope that many others will do so when they hear what he has to say. In this assurance he has distinguished precedents. The Greek poets spoke not only to a whole people but actually for it, and saw themselves not only as its leaders and instructors but as committed and characteristic members of it. They were able to do this because they belonged to small city-states, of which they shared all the trials and disputes and tribulations. The poets of the nineteenth century were not so happily placed. They belonged to large nations, which they could understand only by some happy intuition into dominant moods. They lack the immediate, powerful impact of Greek poetry, in which even the most original and most imaginative ideas have been strengthened by the concern of other men for the same issues, and where the poet's authority is greater because he is in close touch with his people and shares their daily excitements and dangers. In the nineteenth century the poet made concessions to his audience because he could not know as human beings more than an infinitesimal fraction of it, and when he tried to catch a general mood, he had to engage his readers on some point which he believed them to share with him. He might of course judge wrongly, but even if he judged rightly, his response could not fail to be limited and even standardised, just because so many people shared it. When Tennyson wrote 'The Charge of the Light Brigade', both he and a large part of his public agreed that a heroic disaster on this scale called for celebration in song, and into his poem he put his appreciation of the des-

4

perate thrill and the unquestioned heroism of the exploit. When he tactfully reduced the cause of this insane exploit to the words 'Someone had blunder'd', he might in our judgement have shirked the most troubling feature of the whole affair, but he would certainly reflect public opinion that this was no time to distribute open blame, since it might detract from the magnificence of the charge. If Tennyson had any qualms about Lord Raglan or Lord Cardigan or Captain Nolan, he did not express them openly.[3] At a time when the British people sorely needed to feel that its achievements in the recent battle were worthy of its military past, Tennyson gave it what it wanted by turning away from the futility of the carnage to its astonishing revelation of discipline and self-sacrifice.

Yet once we recognise the limits within which poets worked, we can see what they were still free to do. If they accepted a common background, they could still impose their own manner and pattern on familiar sentiments. There was plenty of room for lively invention and apt fancy, and though these might mask something ordinary in the poet's approach, it derived its strength from them. Instead of troubling about first principles, poets took them for granted and applied them with full conviction to individual situations. Indeed one of the claims of political poetry in the later years of the nineteenth century is that it was so sure of its main assumptions that it could apply them to current events with an impressive conviction. Russia provides an illuminating counterpart to Tennyson's poem on the Light Brigade. During the siege of Sebastopol Fedor Tyutchev (1803–73), who was a man of conservative outlook and Panslavist aspirations, was moved by a deep compassion for the sufferings of Russian soldiers in the deadly hardships of the Crimean War. For centuries the consolation offered to the Russians for their miserable existence both in peace and in war was that they belonged to 'Holy Russia'[4] and, though they might have a humble and humiliating lot, they were in this respect privileged above other nations. This belief was held by men in all classes, sometimes with a proud superstructure of

5

metaphysics or mysticism, sometimes dimly and faintly, but always as a solace for what might be demanded from Russians by their rulers. It was a source of pride and comfort to many, and even enemies of the Tsarist régime were not immune from it, though from it they might draw unusual conclusions. Tyutchev, writing in August 1855, put this theme into a deeply touching poem[5] which completely lacks the militant aggressiveness of Tennyson's 'Charge of the Light Brigade'. What concerns him is that Russia, despite its poverty and degradation, is strengthened by the presence of Christ, who himself acts as a humble servant and gives his blessing to the country as he passes through it. Tyutchev's art is more subtle and more delicate than Tennyson's. There is no rhetoric and no exaggeration, and what counts is the devout mood of an unquestioning faith presented with both pathos and majesty. Though the Crimean War was very much in Tyutchev's mind, he does not mention it and gains by setting his subject in a wide horizon. But fundamentally he too exploits a current idea which has a wide circulation, that Russia is a poor and humble land redeemed by the presence of Christ, who shares its poverty and its humility and is the image of soldiers suffering in the war. Tyutchev puts into firm and vivid shape the vague, inchoate thoughts which Russian peasants, fatalistically sunk in their religion, may have had in the trenches of Sebastopol. His insight into the soul of the fighting man is very different from Tennyson's, and his feelings are more tender and more controlled, but both poets are impelled and sustained by emotions which they feel at work around them and to which they respond with ideas with which everyone is at home.

This kind of poetry is inspired by individual occasions, but the further it gets away from them, the better it is; for then it hints at wider issues and at mysteries beyond the present scene. In many poems which Giosuè Carducci (1835–1907) wrote about the Italian Risorgimento he places present events in the perspective of the past and through this enlarges their significance, as if they were the inevitable result of what has happened long before but is only now revealed in its full nature. Though history touched Carducci very deeply, he saw it imaginatively and interpreted its more dramatic episodes as if they were myths that illustrated the fore-ordained course of things. As an Italian patriot he shared the ancient dislike of the House of Hapsburg, but he does not present this directly. Rather, when a suitable occasion arises, he builds on it a myth which embodies an abstract idea in a visible, emotive form. In 1878, some fourteen years after the event which it commemorates, he wrote 'Miramare' on the execution by Juarez of the Emperor Maximilian of Mexico.[6] He is clearly moved by this dismal and humiliating end to an absurd endeavour and reads into it a lesson of far-reaching import. He feels the pathos of the young prince, 'il biondo imperatore', as he sails with his proud blue-eyed bride on their fatal quest, but he sees its consequences as directed by ruthless, unseen powers in Mexico, by the dethroned gods of the Aztecs, who clamour for vengeance on the descendants of Charles V for the conquest and enslavement of their land. Maximilian is drawn to Mexico by demons who thirst for his blood, and he cannot resist them. Carducci catches the imagination by his suggestion that the Aztec gods are still able to carry out their deadly designs, that they belong to Mexico and have a place even in its recent history. Maximilian is shot by the Mexicans because his ancestors have maltreated theirs, and such are the plain facts of the case. The mythical form greatly enhances the poetry, and an otherwise painful story gains a savage grandeur from the hidden vengeance biding its time through the centuries. This is Carducci's personal contribution to a dramatic episode, but he would not have made it if he had not shared the common Italian conviction that the Hapsburgs are doomed to suffer for their long record of misdeeds. He has nothing against Maximilian except that he is a Hapsburg, but that evokes the spirit in which he writes the poem. In his view history brings its own justice, and this is what concerns him.

This dependence on an accepted background, which gives

such help to Tyutchev and Carducci, may be no less important in poets who do not belong to an established majority and might be expected not to share its views. This is true of Gerard Manley Hopkins (1844–99), who, as a Jesuit priest, might look at contemporary events from an uncommon angle. So far as his style reflects his vision, he certainly does, but the style, despite all its richness and originality, often conceals thoughts which are more ordinary. A striking example is 'Tom's Garland', which he wrote in September 1887 about the unemployed. It is in his most tortuous and most elliptic manner and makes its main effect by an abrupt change of theme in the middle. It is not surprising that neither Bridges nor Dixon understood it at a first reading, and we are fortunate to have Hopkins's own elucidation of it. The first part is based on the traditional and, at the time, tenable belief that there is a divinely ordered hierarchy of society, in which everyone has a place and in it derives dignity and honour from the whole. This is an ancient notion, and though Hopkins, as a Roman Catholic, accepts it more literally than others might, many would see nothing wrong in it and would probably feel that, if it is not pressed to extremes, it is no more than a variant on the view of the Anglican Catechism that God is pleased to call everyone to a certain state of life. After stating this Hopkins makes a bold and abrupt change and continues:

> Undenizened, beyond bound
> Of earth's glory, earth's ease, all; no one, nowhere,
> In wide the world's weal; rare gold, bold steel, bare
> In both; care, but share care—
> This, by Despair; bred Hangdog dull; by Rage,
> Manwolf, worse; and their packs infest the age.[7]

Hopkins sees that the dignity of labour, with its rewards and its consolations, its sense of belonging to an ordered system, ceases to have any meaning when a man has nothing to do. This condition he describes with insight and knowledge, dwelling in short stabbing phrases on what such a man misses in happiness and confidence and on what a bestial substitute he gets

8

in their place. Hopkins is compassionate and indignant, and the smouldering words respond to his troubled feelings. He seems to put the responsibility for a disastrous phenomenon on a social scheme which is unable to deal with it, and to some degree this is what he does. In this respect he stands apart from most of his contemporaries, who regarded unemployment as the personal fault of the unemployed. But then he takes a new turn and ends by denouncing the results of enforced idleness on those who suffer from it. His compassion changes into a theory which he gives in his letter of explanation: 'And this state of things, I say, is the origin of Loafers, Tramps, Cornerboys, Roughs, Socialists and other pests of society.' His conclusion to the poem is that, when men have nothing in common with each other except care and anxiety, they go wrong, and for this he condemns them. His anger is real and convincing, and his imagery conveys the brutality which he sees as the direct result of unemployment. In so gentle a man this conclusion comes with uncommon force, and though Hopkins plainly means what he says, he shows himself to be after all a true Victorian, who treats unemployment not as a misfortune but as a vice and judges its victims more by their alleged faults than by their real pathos.

This poetry, of which we have given only a few samples, relies on its emotional impact, to which, sometimes despite ourselves, we cannot but surrender. The range of emotions aroused and set to work is large, but in themselves they are relatively simple and uncompounded and contain few internal incongruities. The nineteenth century allowed far freer displays of emotion in ordinary affairs than would be considered seemly nowadays, and this may to some degree account for the licence given to them. But there is a deeper reason than this. Such emotional indulgence is made much easier by assumptions and beliefs which are not normally disputed. Since these cause no trouble, we do not find that struggle with ideas which sometimes adds to poetry a new dimension of intellectual effort, such as we find in Aeschylus and Dante, in Milton and Hölderlin, but not in the poets with whom we are now dealing. In them ideas and the search for them count for far less than their immediate presentation, which gives an up-to-date appeal to familiar notions as they are applied to new circumstances, but does not probe the validity of the notions themselves. This leaves the poet free to release them in full spate, and, if he does this, there is not very much more for him to do. Since he need spend no time on arguing his basic assumptions or explaining their worth or even trying to formulate them more precisely, he can from the start apply them in their full emotional impact. He may himself be carried away by them, but his first aim is to see that others are. This is characteristic of much poetry in the late nineteenth century, but it is particularly the case with political poetry, which hopes to satisfy a large need and must make allowances for it and try to meet it with a response so powerful that doubts are silenced and the reader is swept along by an impetuous surge of feeling.

Even in the most exposed and obvious positions this art can surprise and delight and overwhelm. Yet it contains the seeds of its own corruption. It often has a didactic purpose, a desire to persuade the public to adopt certain opinions. There is nothing intrinsically wrong in a poet wishing to instruct. Through its enormous career Chinese poetry has consistently claimed the right to do so, even though its claims are often belied by its practice; and in their greatest days the Greeks regarded the poet as a teacher who made grave pronouncements both in general on the relations of gods and men and more specifically on concrete issues in which these relations came to the fore. This kind of instruction succeeds because it is given with passion and conviction, because the poet is driven by his genius to expound matters which mean a very great deal to him. But this is not the case with some public poetry of the nineteenth century. It is in danger of overplaying its part, of making its emotional appeal more violent than strict honesty might allow, and of simplifying facts beyond the point of truth. In the end this discredits its authority and undermines its appeal. Because it relies so much on exciting and exploiting the emotions, they are more important to it than the intelligible matter to which they are attached, and the result is sometimes a discord between what is actually said and the power with which it is enforced. This is notoriously the case with Victor Hugo, who with his magnificent command of rhythm and sentiment has not always something perspicacious or inspiring to say. It is even more the case with his devoted disciple Swinburne, especially in the political poems of *Songs before Sunrise*. He maintains the astonishing rush of words, the galloping rhythms, the enthusiasm for France and Italy, but he is so eager to make the most of everything that in the end we are stupefied. There is indeed an intelligible stream of thought, but it moves at a different level from the hustling, bustling emotions and hardly justifies them or bears any close relation to them. What is true of Hugo and Swinburne is even more true of other poets who, lacking their extraordinary gifts, expose their emptiness at a first reading. This was the fated end of the old public manner. Its practitioners assumed too easily that the contents of a poem did not matter very much if they were enforced with sufficient eloquence, and the result was that poets became easy victims of ideas so vapid that even the public found little attraction in them.

From this stress on the emotions follows a second fault. In appealing so strongly to them political poetry is liable to become cheap or shallow or false. Instead of setting a standard to which readers were expected to conform, poets accommodated themselves to what readers felt or were expected to feel, and in so doing came near to being dishonest with themselves by advocating tawdry, vulgarised sentiments. This is most apparent in the abundant patriotic poetry of the period. Love of country is so instinctive and so real that it is particularly liable to distortion and misrepresentation. Because in the last resort it needs no explanation and no apology, poets and their public tend to dress it up and make it look different from what it really is, and though its forms differ from one age to another, the tradition of it is so strong that it often carries into the present what may have been true in the past but is no longer true now. For the Greeks it was enough that a man should die for his city in battle, and they were usually content to record this without making any comment on it, but the Romans, believing that at least in this respect they were superior to the Greeks, needed more to satisfy their sense of an imperial mission, and it was they, and not the Greeks, who inspired much of the patriotic sentiment in the later part of the nineteenth century. For Horace and Virgil war was sufficiently a reality to justify more or less philosophical considerations of it, but in the long European peace before 1914 it had ceased to have any immediate urgency and the thought of it was kept alive by a variety of subterfuges. The further the memory of war receded, the more the prospect of death in it was romanticised until poetry had little relation to the facts or to any normal feeling about them. In taking over convictions which had been real and relevant to the Romans, the later Victorians and their contemporaries in other countries were untrue to their own experience, and to see how wrong they could be we have only to look at the marching-song which Hopkins, at the height of his powers, wrote in 1885.[8] Not only are its thoughts of a shocking banality, but its sentimental vocabulary and its trivial rhythm show that he wrote it not from any inner compulsion but to satisfy some artificial notion of what such a poem should be. Such work has a social significance. It shows how a prosperous and secure society felt that it was falling short of the standards set by its ancestors, and tried to convince itself that it was capable of noble heroism and invincible power, without knowing what either was. It was a drug, a dream, an escape from facts into consoling fancy. Peace created a gap which had to be filled, and it was filled with phantoms of martial ardour and belligerent virility, but nobody asked what forms these would take in the vastly altered conditions of modern war.

The established manner was not finally destroyed until harsh realities showed it up for the absurdity that it was, and relentlessly truthful witnesses gave their own devastating alternatives to it. But when the final stroke came, it was to an art already so corrupt that it would before long have died of its own inanity. Today it is hard to find a word of truth in the sentimental fantasies of Henry Newbolt or William Watson or in the intoxicated vision of national grandeur which A. C. Benson set forth in the words of 'Land of hope and glory' for Elgar's music. Much the same thing happened outside England. The established manner collapsed because public affairs were too serious to be treated in it, and the process was speeded by the excesses of the public poets. Such performers as Paul Fort in France or Gabriele d'Annunzio in Italy, who strained to pass even the existing limits of national boastfulness, revealed their echoing emptiness and left later generations wondering why they had ever been admired. Truth had been kept for too long out of sight and now forced herself on the public attention. The old form of public poetry had in its day been based on genuine, if limited, beliefs, but it had fallen into the hands of men who lived on dreams derived from other dreams and maintained by myopic complacency. Now slowly a more personal note began to come into poetry, and with it a keener sense of truth. Themes which had hitherto been handled in a strictly public spirit were allowed to have an individual temper not merely in vocabulary and treatment but in the assertion of the poet's personality and private sensibility. First signs of change can just be seen in Rudyard Kipling (1865–1936). Though he was the vociferous apostle of imperialism, he kept some touch with reality, and though he thought that the British had a divinely appointed mission to rule large parts of the world, he devoted much energy and eloquence to deploring how unfitted they were to do so.[9] The change came with no great speed, but its beginnings were apparent in 1910, and soon afterwards it was making itself felt far and wide. Much poetry still clung to the old manner and was not sure of its style or technique, but it had made a start in what was to be a long and contentious process.

13

The process of transformation from the old style into the new can be seen in the treatment of a single public event by two different poets in highly characteristic ways. For the funeral of King Edward VII in 1910 Kipling wrote 'The Dead King' with all the authority and pomp that he could muster. This is undeniably a public poem, at times ponderous, pitched throughout on a single note of unquestioning admiration. Kipling tries to speak for the nation, and the strength of his approach is that he says in the hushed and solemn tones appropriate to a funeral what was said all over the Empire and reiterated in newspapers and sermons and common talk. Kipling, whose gift was to pick up the atmosphere of an occasion and make it his own, felt the dramatic shock of the king's death and wrote as majestically as he could about it. He, who once called Edward a 'corpulent voluptuary', is now on his best behaviour, but it is not a pose, and his words ring true to his convictions. The elegy is also a eulogy, but that after all has many good precedents, and at such a moment there is nothing wrong in being generous to someone who has just died. Though there is a large element of rhetoric in the poem, it is meant not to persuade or to convert but to strike a composed, collected attitude in the presence of death. At the same time Kipling does not say all that he might about Edward's unusual character. His taste for display and for pleasure is not mentioned, though it was probably for his race-horses and his mistresses that the British people liked him as much as it did. In keeping silence on this point Kipling follows the true Victorian tradition, which insists that at such times the best is all that need be said. But though he is wrapped in the solemnity of death, Kipling keeps something of himself and looks at things from his own point of view. It is characteristic of him that what he admires in the dead king is his devotion to his job. With Kipling the job was very much the man, and here it takes precedence over everything else. This was not the only point that could be made, and it was not perhaps so important as Kipling thought. But in making it Kipling speaks from his own admiration, and this tempers his public manner. He has not only used the old style at its best but given it a new direction which we might not have expected from him.

The same theme caught the imagination of Thomas Hardy (1840–1928), who, though he was twenty-five years older than Kipling, was in many ways more up-to-date both as a man and as a poet. In 'A King's Soliloquy' he avoids the public approach and the familiar sentiments by neither praising nor condemning the dead king but making him speak in his own person from beyond the grave and pass a considered verdict on his life. Into this Hardy puts his own tender, detached, ironical view of high position and the price that has to be paid for it. Though, like Kipling, Hardy is keenly aware that Edward VII worked hard at his job, he is not afraid to mention other sides of his character, which were of course known to everyone and contributed to his popularity. Kipling evidently thought that they were inappropriate to the solemn moment, but Hardy finds them indispensable to any estimate of Edward's human qualities:

> I have eaten the fat and drunk the sweet,
>   Lived the life out
> From the first greeting glad drum-beat
>   To the last shout.
>
> What pleasure earth affords to kings
>   I have enjoyed
> Through its long vivid pulse-stirrings
>   Even till it cloyed.[10]

Hardy, more true to himself than to Edward, concludes by making him say that, if he had to live again, he would prefer 'the average track of average men'. We may question whether the king, who had a lively taste for show and ceremony, for uniforms and vast meals, would have agreed with him, but it shows Hardy's strong impulse to impose his own interpretation on this public event. This was what he thought, and it sets the pleasures and toils of kingship in an illuminating perspective. So far from wishing to say the correct, conventional thing

Hardy follows his own inclinations, and his poem is quite as interesting for its point of view as for the calm spirit that pervades it. In their different ways both Kipling and Hardy speak from personal angles, but Hardy is more adventurous and has a more original approach, and in him the break with Victorian manners is more emphatic.

This change of temper was reinforced by the First World War. At its start poets, who as yet knew nothing about war and especially about this war, wrote from attitudes inherited from the past and drifted further and further from reality. They were honest enough, but they were trying to do something which their ignorance made impossible. The inadequacy of their performance was exposed when soldiers, who knew about war from the inside, wrote about it and showed that in no way did it resemble the orthodox picture of it. What engaged them was not the abstract ideas and vague sentiments which propaganda had smeared over it but its unusual moments and sudden surprises in an isolated and fantastic world. They saw that they could not grasp its whole character, and they concentrated on limited effects which they understood from their own experience. Their response was indeed various, but all agreed that, if poetry was to be written about war, it must be about war as the poet knew it. In this they had been anticipated by Arthur Rimbaud (1854–91), who at the age of seventeen had moved on the fringes of the Franco-Prussian War and seen that, if he was to tell the truth about it, he must rely on what he saw and nothing else. Just as in 'Le Mal'[11] he hits off the irony and the confusion of the battlefield with its showy accoutrements, its insensate folly, and its bitter pathos, so in 'Le Dormeur du Val',[12] he describes a dead soldier, who seems to be quietly asleep but has two red holes in his right side. Rimbaud indeed anticipated many of the new shapes which poetry has taken since his time, and this he certainly did for war. The soldier-poets of 1914–18 were, usually without knowing it, his heirs and successors, not merely in their treatment of war but in their whole conception of poetry as a private world which the poet creates for his own satisfaction without troubling whether the public agrees with him or not.

This movement towards the personal treatment of public themes had many aspects, and of course even the most intimate poets could not at times fail to deal with large subjects, if only because they felt compelled to come to terms with them in their own minds and so to master them. The Armistice of 11 November 1918 shows the variety of response which such an event may provoke. It brought an incredible relief even to the defeated, but it was a real event, not an abstract notion or an empty word. It meant the end to haunting fears of death or mutilation, to long years of boredom and filth and exhaustion. This was a subject on which any poet, no matter how austere his conception of his art, might feel himself compelled to write, and nobody would complain if he wrote about what the Armistice meant to him personally, since almost everyone was a victim of the war and could not fail to be relieved by its unexpected end. It is therefore not surprising that Hardy wrote for it a poem 'And there was a Great Calm'. He does not follow his usual, highly individual method of selecting some single significant episode which touches him deeply and suggests many unexpressed possibilities beyond itself. Perhaps he felt too far from actual events to attempt such a method, since such themes were nearly always what he had himself noticed. He attempts instead on a large scale an impression of the sudden silence and calm which the Armistice brings to the vast arena of the battlefields. In this he applies to his own time a device which he has used with much success in *The Dynasts*, when he presents to the imagination the whole of Europe with armies moving over it and fleets sailing across its seas, and now in a more gigantic conflict he tries to take in at one glance what it all means when it ceases. The result is impressive and touching and true. Hardy's compassionate imagination has no difficulty in understanding what war means to those who take part in it. He marks the main facets of his enormous theme and gives to each some percipient, telling touch, and then he comes to his finale:

Calm fell. From Heaven distilled a clemency;
There was peace on earth, and silence in the sky;
Some could, some could not, shake off misery:
The Sinister Spirit sneered: 'It had to be!'
And again the Spirit of Pity whispered, 'Why?'[13]

Hardy speaks for an enormous multitude, and through his very simplicity what he says is relevant to everyone. What is original is his interpretation of what has happened, and though this rises from his own tentative philosophy, which is more myth than metaphysics, it is curiously adequate to such an occasion. Hardy combines his new independence with something of the old stateliness and derives advantages from both.

With this we may compare a very different poem, and the gap between the two illustrates what happened to the younger generation in its revolt against the public poetry of its elders. For the same occasion Siegfried Sassoon (b. 1886), who had himself known and denounced the insane horror of war and suffered for his courage in doing so, wrote a short poem 'Everyone Sang'. He did not indicate what had inspired it, and may not have cared whether his readers guessed it or not. It is totally unlike Hardy's poem and moves in almost a different order of consciousness:

Everyone suddenly burst out singing;
And I was filled with such delight
As prisoned birds must find in freedom,
Winging wildly across the white
Orchards and dark-green fields; on—on—and out of sight.

Everyone's voice was suddenly lifted;
And beauty came like the setting sun:
My heart was shaken with tears; and horror
Drifted away...O, but Everyone
Was a bird; and the song was wordless; the singing
    will never be done.[14]

This is the record of a personal mood, which is not, as in Hardy, of relief but of joy breaking irresistibly into song. This is not, and is not meant to be, the spirit in which soldiers greeted the tremendous silence at 11 a.m. on 11 November 1918 but it is

very much what the poet felt, his unusual, uncontrollable interpretation of the moment. If the first verse conveys the almost
incredible thrill of deliverance, the second moves into endless
distances. The actual song becomes the very spirit of song, and
its effects will never quite pass away. Sassoon is more adventurous than Hardy, who would never indulge in such optimism
or allow so bold a flight of fancy, but this is permissible to
Sassoon, who is young and knows from the inside what the
Armistice means. Only by so bold a stroke can he express what
he feels. Yet though both Hardy and Sassoon speak firmly for
themselves on a large public issue and thereby make it real,
neither perhaps gets quite as much out of it as he might. Hardy's
abstractions are a little remote, and his poem lacks somewhat
the intense compassion of which he is capable in dealing with
smaller themes, while Sassoon so limits himself to a single mood
and keeps even that so simple that he seems to shirk some of his
opportunities. Poets had still some way to go before they could
rise to the full challenge of public events.

The progress of English poetry from a conventional, public
manner to greater truth and keener personal insight has a
counterpart in Russian, where for political reasons the change
began a little earlier. In 1905 Russia suffered the humiliation
of defeat by Japan and in the same year witnessed the first
outbreak of revolution. Though her defeat astonished the whole
world and awoke the darkest forebodings in many high quar-
ters, it did not at first produce any strong reactions in poets at
home. Even the battle of Tsushima, when the Russian fleet,
which had sailed from the Baltic round the Cape of Good Hope
to the China Sea, was sunk in a few minutes by the Japanese,
did not strike unqualified dismay; for an opiate was found in
the belief that Russia was still Holy Russia, God's chosen
country, reserved for a unique, if undescried, destiny. Even the
hard-headed and sophisticated Valery Bryusov (1873–1924),
who wrote of the disaster in a full knowledge of its completeness,
consoled himself with the trust that Russia had not forfeited
her destiny to rule in the Far East or to succeed Byzantium as

the Third Rome.[15] Such rewards may have been postponed but he did not doubt that they would come. Though the notion of Holy Russia might seem to have been discredited by recent events, it was still so canonised in popular belief that it was accepted almost without question and could be applied to almost any circumstances. Russia, like England, still seemed content to look at public events, even of the most disturbing kind, from an established point of view, and though it was enjoying a remarkable revival of poetry after some fifty barren years, it did not for the moment apply its creative powers to new and present needs.

Yet before long the events of 1904 and 1905 brought their results, and poets ceased to be satisfied with the imperial dream. The increasing ineptitude of the tsar and his ministers bred in many Russian poets a mood of increasing anxiety and doubt for their country. Excluded, as most of them were, from any opportunity to give her active service, they turned with all the deeper conviction to the arts and gave them a whole-hearted devotion. Russia was still a dominating reality for them, but they were no longer so sure that she was a Holy Mother. Russian patriotism had long differed from British by the different quality and emphasis of its religious background. Whereas in Great Britain this was largely Protestant and based on the Old Testament with its assurance that, though the Lord may chastise His people for its good, He will not in the end desert it, in Russia it was intimately bound to the Eastern Orthodox Church, which gave sanctity to autocracy and laid much stress on the redeeming quality of suffering. The Russian outlook had long concealed a deep dichotomy between its worldly and its celestial claims, but now events forced this into the open, and the holy mission of Russia was examined with a more critical curiosity. At the same time Russian poets, trying to find new outlets for their religious yearnings, turned to various kinds of mysticism which could somehow be fitted into an Orthodox scheme but allowed plenty of room for adventurous idiosyncrasies. The new wave of Symbolist poets pursued

20

mystical ideals, and chief among these was the belief that in the transfiguration of their country they would find the completion and fulfilment of their prayers. This took various forms, and poets might quarrel with one another about them, but the basic assumptions were the same and had a far more immediate urgency than the old idea of Holy Russia.[16] Led by Vladimir Soloviev (1853–1900) poets really believed that some cosmic revelation was at hand and that Russia would be its first and chief beneficiary. Andrei Bely (1880–1934) found no difficulty in combining such apocalyptic hopes with the anthroposophy of Rudolf Steiner and turned both into poetry in which even the most ordinary matters are lit with all the colours of the rainbow. The Russian Symbolists might agree with one another about the supreme importance of poetry, but their manners were remarkably diverse, and each approached his exalted themes from a strictly personal point of view.

The greatest poet and most inspired visionary of this generation was Alexander Blok (1880–1921). He had been on the side of the frustrated Revolution in 1905 and after losing his first dreams found in love for his country a new centre for his creative being. He passed through many phases in his relations with her, and their ups and downs have the variety of a troubled love affair. At the start he had seen her as something that he could love and serve, and he wanted revolution because he thought it would make her more truly herself. But after 1905 he changed his point of view, and for a time Bely thought that he had abandoned their common cause, and reproached him bitterly for it. But in fact Blok's feelings for Russia were more human and more natural than Bely's and passed through several phases, all of which show how tyrannically she obsessed him. He spoke of her in the language of devoted passion and saw on the field of Kulikovo, where in 1380 Dmitri Donskoy had defeated the Tatar hordes, signs and portents of awakening and glory, but at the same time he tempered all this with a growing insight into her ambiguous character.[17] In 1910 she is still his country and his life, but she is also the embodiment of brutal despotism, conquest, exile, and imprisonment. He addresses her with mocking irony and asks whether she and he ought to part because they are weary of one another and have nothing but regrets for their past relations. He derides her failure to realise her ambitions, to gain the power which she has sought for so long, and especially to capture Constantinople, which is the symbol of her imperial aims.[18] Blok's ambivalent, searching, distrustful attitude is the natural result of the harm done by chicanery and brutality to the old ideal of Russia as a crusading, Christian country. He feels that he is her plaything, that she is a deceitful mirage, and yet that he cannot live without her. He makes no concessions to any public belief and speaks entirely for himself with piercing insight and apocalyptic passion. Between 1905 and 1914 Blok illustrates the remarkable change which had come over Russian poetry on public themes. The old dependence on accepted ideas has been greatly modified, and though some of them are present in a new form, it is not the public but the poet who now decides and dictates what events mean. No compromises are made with convention, and the poet is concerned with truth as he sees it. Russia has become so inextricably part of himself that he speaks of her with a fierce and almost frightening intimacy.

The hopes and forebodings which marked Russian poetry before 1914 were tested first by the war and then by the Revolution. In both of them Russian poets spoke from their own points of view and maintained a remarkable integrity of utterance about events which affected their private lives to an incalculable degree. Once a poet has been stung into song by some public event, his task is to present it as forcefully as he can from his own understanding of it, and this is where the poetry of our times differs most from that of the last century. Its business is to correct the standard forms which events take in the public mind and to give new, illuminating versions of them. If newspapers and common talk choose salient points and give an obvious interpretation of them, the picture so formed is accepted as correct and complete. But the poet must brush this aside and say something true and new and enlightening. From the mass of material he must make his selection and concentrate on the few points which really strike him deeply but need not belong to the public picture, and it may be their very unfamiliarity which gives them a special hold. In December 1916 the murder of Grigori Rasputin by Russian aristocrats was an event that rang round the world. Rasputin was a 'holy man' of infamous habits, who had by his extraordinary gift for healing the young tsarevich in his fits of bleeding won an astonishing ascendancy over the tsar and his devoted, obstinate, and foolish wife. He was murdered because he was thought, justly, to wish to make peace with Germany, and, unjustly, to be likely to persuade the tsar to do so. His resistance to death, after being both poisoned and shot, revealed an almost inconceivable hold on life, and he was not proved to be dead until his body was taken out of the freezing Neva. The theme, dramatic in every detail and worthy of a civilisation in its death-throes, soon took a familiar form and was exciting enough in it, but Nikolai Gumilev (1886–1921) was fascinated by this monstrous being, whom he feared and condemned and yet somehow admired.

The result was his poem 'Мужик' ('Peasant'), in which Rasputin is not named but is immediately recognisable. Gumilev sketches a wild, primeval creature, bred in swamps and forests, communing with pagan gods and akin to barbarous, alien peoples, who keeps company with thieves and finds his recreation in tavern brawls. Then this monster of the wilds does something which nobody could have foreseen and which has incalculable consequences for the whole of Russia:

В гордую нашу столицу
Входит он — Боже, спаси! —
Обворожает царицу
Необозримой Руси

Взглядом, улыбкою детской,
Речью такой озорной, —
И на груди молодецкой
Крест просиял золотой.[19]

*To our proud capital city*
*He comes, and his spell commands*
*The Empress—O God, have pity!—*
*Of Russia's limitless lands*

*With his gaze, with his childlike laughter,*
*And his talk oh so mischievous;*
*And on his huge breast there glitters*
*The shape of a golden cross.*

The inconceivable has happened, and Gumilev speaks of it with awe and wonder and horror. The actual murder of Rasputin is presented indirectly in the image of the stunned capital like a lioness protecting her young, and this conveys its primitive ferocity. But Gumilev's special interpretation comes out in other, more striking ways. First, in his introductory account of Rasputin as a child of the wilds, he magnifies the traditional qualities of a peasant. Rasputin was indeed built on a scale larger and far more unnatural than life, and Gumilev treats him in this way to stress partly the enormous gap which should separate him from the empress, partly his primitive powers and formidable personality. Secondly, Gumilev, who regards Rasputin as a monster, is in his own way fair to him. He gives to him dying words which appeal to the Russian people, ask who will now protect the orphan, and assert that in his country there are many other peasants like himself whose footsteps can be heard tramping on the roads. This is a tribute to the undeniable position of Rasputin as the spokesman of the Russian people and to his own vision of himself in this role, and it contains a menace that more of his kind will appear. Though Gumilev was by caste and conviction on the side of the murderers and understood their motives, he sees the other side of the case and by this gives a fairer and fuller picture of this astonishing episode. It would have been easy to treat it in stereotyped lines, but Gumilev greatly enriches it by his imaginative grasp of what it means.

The independence which Gumilev shows in dealing with this theme was to find ample parallels in poets who were caught by the Russian Revolution and inextricably bound to its fatalities. Their personal quandary enabled them to see it not in black and white but as a complex crisis which deeply affected their lives and to which they were in the last analysis ambivalent. They felt its power and its grandeur, but also its pathos and its horror. Theirs was not the only way of looking at it, but though to some degree they accepted it and did not resist it, this did not prevent them from seeing some aspects of it with a peculiar clarity. In 1919 Osip Mandel'shtam (1892–1938), who stood rather apart from the main currents of Russian poetry and whose quiet, meditative manner was formed in reaction against the grand style of the Symbolists, published his remarkable *Tristia*, and the poem which gives the name to the book catches a mood which may have been common enough but embodies with remarkable force and fidelity Mandel'shtam's own feelings at the time. In it he sets out in quiet, unusual, carefully ordered images the contrast between the hopes raised by the Revolution and the almost numbed consciousness of those who are involved in it. He knows what it means to say good-bye to much that he loves, and this counters and corrects his hopes for something new and splendid. He does not know what future awaits him and is not sure that he wants anything, but he feels expectation in the air, and it both allures and troblues him:

> Кто может знать при слове — расставанье,
> Какая нам разлука предстоит,
> Что нам сулит петушье восклицанье,
> Когда огонь в акрополе горит,
> И на заре какой-то новой жизни,
> Когда в сенях лениво вол жует,
> Зачем петух, глашатай новой жизни,
> На городской стени крылами бьет?[20]

> *Who, when the word 'Good-bye' is being spoken,*
> *Knows what a parting waits for us, what is*
> *The promise that the cock's loud cries betoken*
> *When the fire burns on the Acropolis?*
> *In some new life when fires of dawn are flaming,*
> *When idly chew the oxen in the shade,*
> *Why does the cockerel, new life proclaiming,*
> *Flap on the city's rampart with wings splayed?*

25

Mandel'shtam is ambiguous towards the Revolution because he does not know what will happen, but he remains patient and philosophical as he questions the portents and asks what they mean. This is his personal approach, but it does not prevent him from taking in a whole wide sweep of experience. He sees the situation in its paradoxes and contradictions and from this moves to a much wider plane on which he speaks for thousands who are in the same position as himself.

An almost exact contemporary of Mandel'shtam, Anna Akhmatova (b. 1889), shared his belief in a neat, precise language and was already well known when the Revolution came. She had hitherto written mostly on private matters, especially on love, and this had given her the opportunity to compose poems which may be narrow in their scope but do as much as possible within it. The Revolution drove her to write about larger and more adventurous themes, which she knew about from the inside, since she stayed in Russia, suffered all the hardships of the Revolution and the Civil War, and lost her former husband, Nikolai Gumilev, to a firing-squad in 1921. Her earlier poetry prepares the way for her later, and her poems about Russia have the uncertainties of a passionate entanglement, with its hopes and its torments, its changes of mood and of circumstance. She responds to the immediate moment and in her questioning candour is driven from one position to another. In 1917 she uses the language of love for a political theme and complains that everything is forbidden to her and that she is shut off alike from Paradise and from Hell.[21] In 1919, when things were at their worst in Russia and the bare struggle for survival was almost intolerably hard, she maintains her dignity and looks at the situation with some detachment, but cannot fail to see that the outlook is indeed forbidding:

> Чем хуже этот век предшествующих? Разве
> Тем, что в чаду печали и тревог
> Он к самой черной прикоснулся язве,
> Но исцелить ее не мог.

Еще на западе земное солнце светит,
И кровли городов в его лучах блестят,
А здесь уж белая дома крестами метит
И кличет воронов, и вороны летят.[22]

*Is our time worse than all the times that went before it,*
*Except that in the frenzy of its anxious grief*
*It touched the blackest of our sores and wished to cure it*
*But had no strength to bring relief?*

*There, in the West, Earth's sun still shines serene and steady,*
*And in its setting glow the roofs are glittering;*
*But here Death marks the houses with a cross already,*
*And calls the ravens on. Ravens are on the wing.*

Though the mention of the West fits easily into the imagery of the evening, it has an ulterior reference to the state of Europe outside Russia, and by this small touch Akhmatova sets Russia in a large perspective. Yet the mood of 1919, which is truly reflected in this poem, was to pass, and by 1921 Akhmatova had formed a more considered judgement on the new state of affairs, but even this contains contradictions. At one moment she complains that she is the slave of a savage master, who keeps her in his den, teaches her humility, and drills her until she calls to a passer-by for help.[23] This is how she sees the discipline of the Leninist state, and though she speaks from her own angle, she is by no means alone in it. Yet at almost the same moment she reveals the ambivalence of her outlook. She knows that all has been betrayed, looted, and sold, but there is in the air a scent of cherries from unknown orchards and new constellations have risen in the sky.[24] However ghastly the present may be, she cherishes a hope that the future will bring new and better things, and this too is true to herself and her time.

Yet Akhmatova's trouble is that she can never quite forget the past, and that, though it has gone for ever, its memory haunts her. Too much of herself belongs to it, and in 1923 in the image of Lot's wife she conveys the ambiguous character of her grief. She knows that Lot was led by God from Sodom, but she cannot help feeling a deep sympathy for his wife, who takes a last look at the place where she has been a bride and borne her sons:

Взглянула, и, скованы смертною болью,
Глаза ее больше смотреть не могли,
И сделалось тело прозрачною солью,
И быстрые ноги к земле приросли.

Кто женщину эту оплакивать будет?
Не меньшей ли мнится она из утрат?
Лишь сердце мое никогда не забудет
Отдавшую жизнь за единственный взгляд.[25]

*She turned back to look, but was frozen by anguish*
*Of death, and her eyes could no longer see;*
*Her body was turned into salt, and imprisoned*
*By earth were her feet, as she sought to go free.*

*Is there nobody who will shed tears for this woman?*
*Or feel for her loss and the choice that she took?*
*In my heart alone she shall not be forgotten,*
*Who gave up her life for the sake of one look.*

Akhmatova's conflicts change as the Revolution recedes and the new order is more firmly established. She accepts the present, regrets the past, and has no fine hopes for the future. She is able to take in the whole situation and to decipher its meaning, and in this her deep personal commitment sharpens her insight. Though the Revolution has treated her hardly, she has not lost her sense of reality, but deepens and extends it as she tries to grasp what the vast changes in the world mean. No preconceived opinion shapes her art. She speaks from her sensibility and her suffering, and this does not in any way diminish the range of her vision.

In these Russian poets, as in Hardy and Sassoon, changes in outlook and attitude were not matched by any parallel changes in technique. On the whole they tend to use modified or refined versions of forms which have long been established and to maintain a traditional regularity and ease of movement and a vocabulary free from neologisms or slang. Within these limits their work is highly accomplished and effective; they choose their words with a fine discrimination and their details are as secure as their total effect. But of course there is much that this kind of poetry cannot do. Just because it is regular and rhythmical, it cannot fully reflect chaotic or erupting moods; because it employs an educated speech, it may lack something in forcefulness; because it keeps its imagery within accepted bounds, it is never explosive. Yet this is just what some younger poets now wished to be. They felt an overpowering conviction that poetry was too tame for the events with which it had to deal, and that what it needed was not reform but revolution. So in this period, while political poetry was gaining a new strength by rejecting the old spirit, revolutionary poets wanted something more, and bold pioneers attempted to transform their craft and make it represent more truly and more fully the feelings of a generation all too conscious of its uncertainty and its disorder. In Russia, while Blok was at the height of his powers writing apocalyptically in a rich language with a full command of formal verse, a younger poet was already at work fashioning highly original methods to express his militant distaste for the existing situation. In 1912, at the age of nineteen, Vladimir Mayakovsky (1893–1930), who had already served three sentences in prison for subversive activities, wrote a short piece 'Я' ('I'). It is in the new futurist manner and seeks to surprise and to shock, but it conveys the feelings of a young man who sees his whole world as a gaol:

> По мостовой
> моей души изъезженной
> шаги помешанных
> вьют жестких фраз пяты.
> Где города
> повешены
> и в петле облака
> застыли
> башен
> кривые выи, —
> иду
> один рыдать,
> что перекрестком
> распяты
> городовые.[26]

*On the pavement*
*of my trampled soul*
*the steps of madmen*
*weave the prints of rude crude words.*
*Where cities*
*hang*
*and in the noose of cloud*
*the towers'*
*crooked spires*
*congeal—*
*I go*
*alone to weep*
*that crossroads*
*crucify*
*policemen.*

The political background has receded out of sight and yet it is fully at work in the poet's consciousness. He sees the city of St Petersburg as a gallows and the towers as corpses dangling from it. He breaks into 'rude crude words' from the oppressive feeling of imprisonment which obsesses him. The poem has a savage pathos, which strikes almost a new note. Mayakovsky treats everything as a scene of persecution and death, in which even the policemen are tortured. This is pre-eminently a personal view, but before long others were to share it and help to create that radical change in the matter and form of poetry which has marked the last fifty years.

Mayakovsky's example shows that the new manner, despite its eruptive subjectivity, is quite prepared to handle large themes. He himself spoke for the oppressed majority of the Russian people under a political system which offered neither comfort nor hope. His experimental style was well fitted for revolt and complaint and perfectly apt for moods which did not fall into the regular manner of a more conventional style. He and his kind were the antithesis of optimistic patriots, and, though in a strange way they loved their country, they viewed its future with anxiety and alarm. One of their chief weapons was an ability to compress a bursting power into a small space. This spirit of revolt and its accompanying mannerisms were not confined to Russia, but were a European phenomenon enforced by conditions which drove talented men into despondency and despair. In the very darkness of their gloom they were able to take an embracing view of their world. So the Austrian Georg Trakl (1887–1914) suffered from a melancholy consciousness that his country was in full decay and had no prospects for the future, but his pessimism extended beyond it to western Europe, of whose chances he writes in 'Abendländisches Lied' ('Song of the Western Countries'). Just before the outbreak of the First World War he compares the bleak present with the radiant past and concludes with a gloomy forecast for the future. In his concentrated, elliptic style the meaning of every word must be pressed, and we can see how deeply he feels the moribund condition of Europe. Yet at the end he offers some sort of consolation:

> O, die bittere Stunde des Untergangs,
> Da wir ein steinernes Antlitz in schwarzen Wassern beschaun.
> Aber strahlend heben die silbernen Lider die Liebenden:
> Ein Geschlecht. Weihrauch strömt von rosigen Kissen
> Und der süsse Gesang der Auferstandenen.[27]

> *O, the bitter hour of defeat,*
> *When we see a stony face in black waters.*
> *But, spreading light, lovers lift their silver eyelids:*
> *A single body. Incense streams from pillows of roses*
> *And the sweet song of those risen from the dead.*

Trakl faces a huge issue, which he first simplifies, and then presents with disturbingly evocative symbols. His thesis is that the present, despite its failures and its forebodings, still draws comfort from living youth and from what has survived of lasting value from the past. He sets this out very much in his own way, but his mood and even his directing idea belong to the age in which he wrote. In him a deep concern for the Western world prompts a truly imaginative and imaginatively truthful vision of what the present means between the past and the future.

These poems by Mayakovsky and Trakl were written before the outbreak of the First World War and show how far the change in political poetry had gone. The war did much to speed the process, and at the end of it poets looked on it with very different eyes from what they had at its start. For the more troubled among them the new manner offered opportunities which seemed beyond the reach of the old melodious style, and just as Guillaume Apollinaire used free verse for some of his brilliant poems of the battlefield, so after the war a sharp, disillusioned spirit faced large issues as they now forced themselves on the attention. In 'Pour l'élection de son sépulchre' Ezra Pound depicts a typical man of his generation with his disappointments and his frustrations and in the last section passes a verdict on the war in which so many men of this kind were killed:

> There died a myriad,
> And of the best, among them,
> For an old bitch gone in the teeth,
> For a botched civilisation,
>
> Charm, smiling at the good mouth,
> Quick eyes gone under earth's lid,
> For two gross of broken statues
> For a few thousand battered books.[28]

The free verse, derived ultimately from Rimbaud, matches the sharp, conversational tone, and both are new arrivals in English literature, though the first signs of them could have been seen in 1910. The old Italianate ease, which had ruled since the seventeenth century, has been abandoned for something harsher and more irregular, as befits an unprecedented situation. The disillusion of the post-war world called for a new style, and this is what it got. The Georgian manner, which was an attempt to purify the Victorian style by removing some of its archaisms and affectations, was not powerful enough to respond to the new, acrid moods, but Pound saw what was needed and wrote his epitaph on the war with uncompromising candour and no concessions to accepted canons of good taste. In 1908 J. M. Synge had written 'It may almost be said that before verse can be human again it must learn to be brutal'[29] and now some ten years or so later his prophecy was fulfilled, as poets throughout Europe, recovering painfully from the shocks of war and revolution and determined not to be deceived by discredited catchwords, set down their feelings exactly as they observed them.

This transformation of attitude and manner has not made the poet's task easier. The old conventions, now useless and abandoned, at least indicated what tone and temper he should adopt for a public theme, but now he must follow his own instinct and speak from his own insight. Much of his work has necessarily been tentative and experimental, but its virtues are those of a searching and self-critical art. If we try to look at the whole picture in its main lines, we see an intricate but not indecipherable pattern, in which three separate forces are at work. First, the reassertion of poetical integrity, which began in France and spread forcefully over Europe, means that any serious political poetry must take account of purely poetical values and nothing else. It must eschew rhetoric and make no concessions to public opinion just because it is public opinion. It must not be a means of indoctrination, nor must it present a manufactured point of view in order to make itself more impressive. Secondly, public and political themes, which elicit a wide range of response, must not be penned in artificial boundaries but appear in their natural richness and authenticity, even though they contain bizarre, horrifying, squalid, or ludicrous elements. Thirdly, the modern emphasis on the poet's obligation to be true to his own vision and sensibility means that, even when he deals with large concerns and complex ramifications, he must handle them in his own way, from his own angle, with his own unique insight. In the last fifty years each of these tendencies has been busily at work and has developed its own limitations and conflicts. No problem in poetry can ever have a final solution, and the problems raised by political poetry are no exception to this rule. We must take it as we find it and ask what poets have tried to do and how far they have succeeded in doing it.

CHAPTER 2

# PROPHETS AND SEERS

In undeveloped societies poetry and prophecy are so closely connected that it is almost impossible to distinguish between them. The singer reveals to other men what he has learned from a supernatural source, and he is both a poet and a prophet in that he uses the technique and the concentration of poetry to give power to his prophecies and believes that he is literally inspired. The finest poetry of the Hebrews was that written by their prophets, who were political and religious leaders and regarded, alike by themselves and by others, as mouthpieces of the jealous national god. Their prestige gave them a unique authority, and this accounts for the superb confidence with which they spoke about the affairs of the people of Israel. If they watched anxiously over its religious and moral welfare, they watched no less anxiously for the many enemies who threatened it and were often too powerful for it. If they chid their own people for its shortcomings and infidelities, they pro- phesied doom for its enemies and exulted with unfeigned savagery when Moab or Nineveh or Babylon fell to rivals as brutal as itself. Yet despite the influence of the Old Testament on Europe since the Reformation, prophetic poetry on the Hebrew model has been rare. Poets have in most times made forecasts of things to come, but on the whole they have not assumed the majestic manner or claimed the supernatural authority of prophets. Even Shelley's Utopian forecasts were based on what he believed to be rational calculations, and though Swinburne used the language of the Bible to denounce its beliefs, he was in no sense a prophet. Until recent years the one authentic prophet-poet in the English language was William Blake, who lived among visions, of which the authors were in eternity, and who used the dark symbols of a private religion to hearten or warn or denounce his countrymen. He

34

is the true type of the prophet in the modern world, but though he had a considerable influence on poets from the nineties onwards, he did not shape their outlooks. Those of them who took to prophecy did so from a powerful urge in themselves, and though they are to be found in more than one country, they are not the pupils of a single master but the products of an intellectual situation which calls for some attention.

In the first decade of this century prophetic poetry assumed a pre-eminence such as it never had before in Europe. It was indeed not to be found in Latin countries, perhaps because the Catholic Church carried out its immemorial task of delivering forecasts and menaces and spoke with an authority which brooked no rival. But in the British Isles, Germany and Russia the prophet-poet held the centre of the stage and handled subjects of vast import with a far greater insight and conviction than the wildest Romantics were ever capable of. He was fully conscious that he had something very special to say, and he said it with a power and majesty worthy of his supernatural claims. William Butler Yeats (1865–1939) may indeed have learned something from Blake, but he learned more from Irish folk-lore and age-old beliefs in hidden powers behind the visible scene, and perhaps most of all from his conviction that his own imaginative insight was much too vivid to be dismissed as a subjective idiosyncrasy. He developed the air, the accents, and the appearance of a prophet, and delivered his messages with a full sense of their urgent relevance to the world. He searched time and space and saw present events in a vast context, and it is precisely this quality which makes prophet-poets so formidable. In Germany Friedrich Nietzsche (1844–1900), whose own too scanty poetry foreshadowed much that was to come, was the forerunner and the master of a whole generation which resembled Yeats, if not in actual power, at least in the claims which it made for the poet's unique knowledge and understanding. Nietzsche looked back to Greek antiquity and especially to its more primitive and less rational sides, and this strengthened his contempt for the modern world and his desire to find remedies for its ills. In Russia Blok and his contemporaries never doubted that they were agents of a divine spirit which enabled them to see what was concealed from most men and to examine the whole scheme of things with an inspired sympathy. This prophetic conviction gave to poetry an extraordinary confidence; in an age of doubt and misgiving it enabled it to speak with complete assurance. It stretched the imagination to the utmost and encouraged it to shrink from no theme however forbidding. It took wings into a menacing empyrean, and poets delivered their messages from remote Sinais. The grand manner had returned in a new shape with far more formidable resources, and poetry, which was drifting into domestic elegance and triviality, again claimed the whole of existence as its field.

The prophet-poet is free to speak with a lofty detachment in his own personal voice. He need not belong to any recognisable group in thought or belief, nor need he be an adherent of any established system of religion or ethics. He is at liberty to develop his own idiosyncrasies. He takes full advantage of this, and though he cannot quite claim divine authority, he can come very near to it in his assertion of inspired insight. Much of his power comes from his being in reaction against the scientific spirit, which is the driving force of our century. Like many others, he seeks to escape from the bleak, uncomforting conclusions of science to what touches the heart, and both his visions and his methods are not so much unscientific as antiscientific. In his system the moment of illumination counts for much more than any process of proof or argument, and in this he runs counter to the brisk assumptions of a pragmatic age. Yet not for nothing does he belong to the ancient tradition of prophets, with whom, despite his peculiarities, he has much in common. He claims an extraordinary authority, which may be based on no more than his private vision, but since he regards this as of transcendent importance, his confidence is unassailable. He sees transitory events in the light of supernatural laws, which may or may not be ascribed to God but have a final influence on human destiny. This means that his poetry has a far more exalted quality than any public utterances of the nineteenth century. His inspired tension raises passing events to an impressive sublimity and convinces us that there is much more in them than we could ever have found for ourselves. In the break-up of the old system this prophetic poetry answered new needs, and though it was not the only answer, it was the most original and the most striking.

The character of this poetry was largely shaped by the Aesthetic Movement, which burst so unexpectedly into prominence in the last years of the nineteenth century. For its adherents the cult of the Beautiful was itself a religious activity, a substitute for faiths which had lost their relevance, a system of life which insisted on the highest ideals of artistic achievement and called for ungrudging efforts to put them into effect. It did an enormous lot for poetry by cleansing it of many feeble and prosaic elements, and it improved craftsmanship beyond reckoning. But as a way of life it had an inherent defect. The cult of the Beautiful ceases to be exalting as soon as the Beautiful is sought in a vacuum without reference to other absolutes. It then turns into a search for sensations, which inevitably become more violent as the jaded palate craves for stronger stimulants. The wiser apostles of the Aesthetic doctrine understood this and anchored their search for the Beautiful on other, more solid beliefs, but even they were not always free of its peculiar influence and responded unconsciously to some of its more doubtful claims. The Aesthetic Movement was a criticism of contemporary society and often spoke of it with horror and disgust. To its adherents the whole achievement of the industrial revolution was a matter for lamentation, the idea of progress a mirage, the destruction of ancient habits and standards the prelude to an odious uniformity. Against the appalling actual scene, with its hypertrophied cities and its multitudes drilled into a grim poverty, it set its withdrawal into a realm of ideal beauty, but in doing this it had to adjust itself to reality, and the adjustment was often painful. The artist might wish to live in a porcelain pagoda, but for his art he must find his material somewhere, and he could not ignore the world outside. He must clarify his attitude to it, and the result was both logical and violent. The aesthetic poets were in conflict with common men, and from this conflict they fashioned some remarkable poetry which attempts to grasp a whole new situation and to speak the essential truth about it.

In Russia, where European movements tend to take a more extreme form than elsewhere, the aesthetic reaction to modernity was vociferous early in the century. A characteristic and influential example is a poem published in 1906 by the Symbolist poet Vyacheslav Ivanov (1865–1949). Ivanov was a classical scholar and a deeply religious man, but neither his youthful training under Mommsen in Berlin nor his lifelong concern with the Christian religion hampered him from writing a poem which claims complete liberty for the artist and emphasises that this will inevitably cause destruction. His aim is to startle and disturb the slothful society around him, and he tells artists what they are to do:

> И с вашего раздолья
> Низриньтесь вихрем орд
> На нивы подневолья,
> Где раб упрягом горд.
>
> Топчи их рай, Аттила, —
> И новью пустоты
> Взойдут твои светила,
> Твоих степей цветы![1]

> *Hurl from your flooding numbers*
> *Your hordes in hurricanes*
> *Where the low valley slumbers*
> *And slaves are proud of chains.*
>
> *Trample their Paradises,*
> *Attila, waste anew!*
> *And where your bright star rises,*
> *The steppe will bud for you.*

In later life Ivanov denied that this poem had any social significance and insisted that it referred only to the freedom of the artist in his own sphere, but this is not what it says. At the very least it is a claim for the artist to destroy in order that he may create, and it demands for him an absolute freedom of action which cannot but be displayed in spheres other than his art, because it is from these that he derives his inspiration and his strength. Ivanov claims a very special position for the artist and sees no reason to explain why he does. He is so sure of it that he issues a manifesto of creative policy which is at once magnificent and frightening.

Whatever private reservations Ivanov may have had about this poem, they were not shared by his contemporaries. Very soon after its publication Valery Bryusov wrote his 'Грядущие Гунны' ('The Coming Huns'), which in its epigraph quotes from it and develops the theme on a large scale, making the most of its alarming possibilities. Bryusov is among the first European poets who in their bitter discontent with their time called for some huge catastrophe to cleanse and change the world. He picks up Ivanov's appeal to Attila and finds in the Huns destroyers after his own heart. They are to come from undiscovered haunts in the Pamir and give new life to withered bodies with their free and fiery blood. Like Ivanov, Bryusov speaks as an aesthete, but as a disillusioned aesthete, whose disillusion turns into lust for a cosmic revolution. All books should be burned and the past annihilated, and though he puts some trust in a few wise men who will preserve the truth in catacombs, deserts, and caves, and hopes that something may be saved, he is not very sure that it will, and in the end it is not clear that he wishes it. What he demands is destruction, almost for its own sake, and he accepts this even for himself:

И что, под бурей летучей,
Под этой грозой разрушений,
Сохранит играющий Случай
Из наших заветных творений?

Бесследно все сгибнет, быть может,
Что ведомо было одним нам,
Но вас, кто меня уничтожит,
Встречаю приветственным гимном.[2]

39

*And what, when the hurricane's raving*
*In the murderous thunderstorm,*
*Will the gamester Chance be saving*
*From the secret shapes that we form?*

*Past tracking, it may be, will perish*
*What alone of the living we knew;*
*But the death that you bring me I cherish,*
*And my hymns give a welcome to you.*

In his desire for an annihilating cataclysm Bryusov, the arch-aesthete, is willing to sacrifice even his art.

Though we might with some justice argue that Bryusov, despite his undoubted power, was a sensationalist who liked to make the flesh creep, and that this poem is not truly representative of its time or of any predominating mood, this is not true. What Bryusov desired from a surfeit of aesthetic sensations other men foresaw with more responsible intentions. In the first years of this century the unexampled increase of material prosperity fostered a nagging suspicion that things were becoming too easy and that sooner or later something disastrous would happen. This had been the mood of Kipling's 'Recessional' and was natural enough as a warning against too complacent a sense of security. Since it was prompted by moral rather than by aesthetic considerations, it is touched by a conviction of guilt which calls for redemption and rebirth. This was to come through bloodshed, and the coarse relaxations of a privileged society were to be paid for by destruction. This was one side of a complex situation, and it certainly owed something to Nietzsche. Though he has been grossly misrepresented, he certainly had a loathing and contempt for his age and believed that what is called civilisation is an unnatural attempt to subdue the natural powers of man and as wrong as trying to tame a wild animal like the lion, 'the magnificent blond beast that prowls in search of booty and victory'.[3] In this Nietzsche protested against the dull uniformity of his time, regarding it as the morality of slaves. Yet though he denounced the present and called for a revival of primitive instincts and especially of courage, making his Zarathustra say: 'I give you this law:

"Make yourselves hard!"',[4] he was not a prophet of inevitable ruin but hoped for the emergence of a new class of supermen, who would have the strength to follow their passions without the self-repression and moderation for which he blamed alike Plato and Christianity. Nietzsche was fundamentally an aesthete like Ivanov and Bryusov, but his aestheticism went far beyond the cult of art and became a system of life. He put all his trust in the creative urge, the free play of desires, the variety and vigour of an artist's life. If he brought not peace but a sword, it was because he believed that this was the only way to restore life to the world.

Nietzsche's doctrine grew from frustration and discontent, and that was why it appealed to many both inside Germany and outside it. Stefan George (1868–1933), who admired him, was much concerned with the regeneration of German youth in the gaudy and gilded age of William II. He hoped so to educate a few chosen disciples that to his spiritually maimed country they would bring the abundance and the spontaneity of Greece and Italy. He hoped to do this first by poetry, especially his own, and it was this sense of a mission that gave strength to his earlier books. So far he was a true son of the Aesthetic Movement, but his aestheticism turned into morality, and the artist into a teacher. In the end his influence was not very great, and his carefully indoctrinated circle had begun to break up before Hitler dealt it a final blow by filching and defiling its catchwords. Though George never wavered in his ideal of 'Kultur', he saw more and more clearly that it was impossible to attain, and that it was not by such means that the sick world was to be healed. Even before 1914 he was demanding a holy war,[5] and though he may have spoken metaphorically, he certainly called for some vast and violent purification, in which tens of thousands were to be stricken by a divine madness. He began by being less ruthless than Nietzsche, but in him too the aesthetic outlook so changed that it almost ceased to deal with aesthetics. Towards the end of his life George was willing to accept some bleak simplification of society in order to get rid of all that he had come to loathe. He had started full of hope, but in the end he became a prophet of destruction.[6]

Once Nietzsche had released his bold imaginations on the world, they could be made to suit convictions which he himself never entertained, and this was what the German Expressionists did. They owed much to him in their prophetic manner and accepted much in his diagnosis of a sick society, but they drew quite different conclusions. They did not wish for a catastrophe; they simply foresaw one. Trakl, an Austrian who understood the decay of his country and saw no cure for it, says in 'Der Abend' ('The Evening'):

> So bläulich erstrahlt es
> Gegen die Stadt hin,
> Wo kalt und böse
> Ein verwesend Geschlecht wohnt,
> Der weisse Enkel
> Dunkle Zukunft bereitet.[7]

> *The moon shines with so blue a light*
> *Over the City,*
> *Where a decaying generation*
> *Lives cold and evil—*
> *A dark future prepared*
> *For the pale grandchild.*

Trakl did not prophesy falsely. His country was indeed to be ruined by the war, which he foresaw, and he himself died of an overdose of drugs on the eastern front, where he was a doctor working with grossly inadequate resources. The city of which he writes in so remote and yet so disturbing a way is his symbol for his age, and he cannot believe that the situation will do anything but get worse. When the war came, he found no satisfaction in knowing that he was right, and in his last poem 'Grodek' he insists that death is not the worst thing brought by war. What is even more terrible is the children who will not be born, and that is his last comment.[8]

Almost contemporary with Trakl was Georg Heym (1887–1912), who was drowned while skating at the age of twenty-five. If Trakl regarded modern cities as seats of spiritual empti-

ness, Heym regarded them as plague-spots of evil on a pro-
digious scale. He sees mankind as driven by uncontrollable
forces to work its own doom, and urban civilisation as caught
by a destiny which it cannot escape. His forecasts of war are
prophetic in the strictest sense, and his vision of a vast holocaust
of human lives was to be fulfilled to the letter. He has a horrifying insight into the decay of human vitality and spiritual
values, and all this he presents in images of lunatics, invalids,
and suicides. His emphatic, highly charged, often harsh and
grating manner is well fitted to what he has to say, and his
nightmare figures are the true reflection of his anxiety-haunted
mind:

> Selbstmörder gehen nachts in grossen Horden,
> Die suchen vor sich ihr verlornes Wesen,
> Gebückt in Süd und West, und Ost und Norden,
> Den Staub zerfegend mit den Armen-Besen.[9]

> *All night huge hordes of suicides go forth,*
> *Men who pursue the selves that they have lost;*
> *Crookbacked they haunt south, west, and east, and north,*
> *And with their arms for brooms they sweep the dust.*

Heym's mood is characteristically German in its deadly concentration on its subject and its acceptance of a historical
inevitability in coming events. Yet in his essential outlook, in
his dark disquiet and his prognostications of doom, he is a child
of his age. The enormous expansion of wealth in the peaceful
years between 1870 and 1914 brought not happiness but fear,
and fear so powerful that it could be expressed only in images
of decay and destruction. When war came, it was almost uni-
versally accepted as something long foreseen and foretold. Even
those who loathed the notion of it acquiesced in it as inevitable,
and it is not foolish to conclude that what ultimately brought
the war was not the uncertain rivalries of European powers, nor
even the ambitions and fears of Germany, but a death-wish in
the peoples of Europe, a half-conscious desire to break away
from their humdrum or horrifying circumstances to something
more exciting or more exalted.

The belief in a coming catastrophe was in wide circulation

43

in Europe, and though it was rare in England, there is more than a hint of it in Kipling with his fears for the end of British power and his denunciation of all who did not live up to his stiff, stern gospel of manhood. The notion spread afield early, for in 1904 the Greek poet, Constantine Cavafy (1868–1933), who lived in Alexandria, was well aware of it, and turned it to his own unique and complex ends. In Περιμένοντας τούς βαρβάρους ('Waiting for the Barbarians'),[10] he sets an imaginary scene in a capital city in the last years of the Roman Empire. A large, excited crowd gathers, and we hear that they are waiting for the Barbarians, who are due to arrive. They are not in the least afraid of the Barbarians. In fact they rather despise them, but no doubt, like other deluded people in more recent times, think that they can manage them. The programme is worked out to suit the tastes of the Barbarians. The Senate is not in session making laws, because, when the Barbarians come, they will make them. The emperor in his crown is seated at the city-gate, with an address, full of names and titles, which he proposes to give to the leader. The consuls and the praetors, clothed in red togas and resplendent jewels, carry their carved walking-sticks, because the Barbarians will be dazzled by the display. On the other hand no orators have come out, because the Barbarians do not like speeches and speech-making. So far Cavafy presents in a convincing historical setting the mood in which an effete people can welcome, almost with excitement, the prospect of barbarian domination. They feel that they themselves are superior, but they are prepared to adapt their habits and hope to get something out of it. This is the first part of the poem, and it deals sharp blows alike at those, like Bryusov, who believe that redemption can be found in a barbarian conquest, and at those, like Heym, who foresee nothing but death and horror. Cavafy's picture is of a lifeless, decadent, profoundly cynical society, and he does not spare it. So far, by setting his scene in a perfectly possible past, Cavafy directs his acid criticism against those who welcome some barbarian revolution and suggests that it is far more likely to come as he foresees it than as they do. The fierce or hysterical hopes started by Nietzsche and developed in different ways by others are punctured by Cavafy's flat realism. He rubs in the theme

Γιατὶ οἱ βάρβαροι θὰ φθάσουν σήμερα,

*Because the Barbarians are arriving today,*

and as this provides the climax of each stanza, it has a hypnotic effect well suited to what the infatuated citizens feel.

At this point Cavafy abruptly changes his tone and his theme. The excitement has suddenly faded, and there is uneasiness and confusion. People's faces become serious, and the streets and squares empty as the people go home full of thought. Then we hear the explanation:

Γιατὶ ἐνύχτωσε κ' οἱ βάρβαροι δὲν ἦλθαν.
Καὶ μερικοὶ ἔφθασαν ἀπ' τὰ σύνορα,
καὶ εἶπανε πὼς βάρβαροι πιὰ δὲν ὑπάρχουν.

Καὶ τώρα τί θὰ γένουμε χωρὶς βαρβάρους;
Οἱ ἄνθρωποι αὐτοὶ ἦσαν μιὰ κάποια λύσις.[10]

*Because night is here, and the Barbarians have not come.*
*And some people have come from the Frontier,*
*Who said that there are no Barbarians any more.*

*And now what will become of us without Barbarians?*
*These people were some sort of a solution.*

Despite the paradox and the irony and the cynical manner Cavafy is entirely serious. He first demonstrates how the desire to be conquered by Barbarians really works, and in this he pictures the vacuity, complacency, and conceit of a civilisation which has lost its sources of vitality and hopes to get others from outside; then he shows that in spite of everything such a desire, however eagerly men may feel it and hope through it to shed their responsibilities, may not be fulfilled, that the hope placed in the Barbarians is itself an illusion, and that things will go on as before in their old, empty way. His people have believed that something will happen; now they find that it will not, and they are gloomy and disappointed. Cavafy punctures a powerful notion current in his time and comes near to discrediting it. His own pessimistic view of civilisation in its

45

decline does not prevent him from distrusting its other critics, who see it in a more lurid light than he does, and though he assumes no prophetic airs but keeps a studied, flat-toned realism, his treatment of the subject is a kind of anti-prophecy, a cold wind let into the heated air of oracular shrines.

Yet, though Cavafy had common sense on his side, it was not he but the prophets who were right. When war broke out in 1914, it was indeed a fulfilment of many prognostications, an answer to many desires and many fears. Its unforeseen brutality and the chaos which it created everywhere made it difficult to apply the prophetic mood which had in advance gained so much from it. Bryusov indeed, who had looked forward to some enormous catastrophe, began by welcoming the war and saw in it a return to the days of Charles Martel, but he was not convincing and perhaps not convinced. George almost seems to have felt that he had been cheated, that though he had wanted some sort of struggle and cleansing, it was not at all what he got, and he retired into the warmth of a few personal friendships, seeing himself as the lonely seer whose words have not been heard and who can do nothing but retire into his own fastnesses as he watches the collapse of his life-work. Blok faced the facts with more courage and wrote, almost in agony, of the darkness which encircled him everywhere. He saw nothing to cheer him in the bleak prospects and at times felt that the world had gone mad, at other times that, though some brilliant revelation might be at hand, he himself might not have the strength to face it. He saw the war as lasting for ever and adding daily to the monotonous toll of suffering and death. It was almost the last phase of his emotional entanglement with Russia, and though it turned his old distrust of her to compassion, he could not believe that any good could come of it. Men actually at the front had little time to consider the further implications of the enormous confusion in which they were caught, and few of them wrote about other matters than the immediate scene which called for all their attention. Yet among these one or two sought to interpret the wider aspects of the slaughter. The

Russian Viktor Khlebnikov (1885–1922) fought as a private soldier on the eastern front and was well aware of its visible aspects, which he recorded with a relentless realism, but also saw it as an eruption of pre-Christian gods, whose savagery and indifference were the real cause of it. He saw them at work in the cruelty of nature and the pathetic contrivances of man, and set out in six lines with a strange magic his fatalistic acceptance of what was happening to the world:

> Годы люди и народы
> Убегают навсегда,
> Как текучая вода.
> В гибком зеркале природы
> Звезды — невод, рыбы — мы,
> Боги — призраки у тьмы.[11]

> *Peoples, years and every creature*
> *In an endless river go,*
> *As the passing waters flow.*
> *In the supple glass of nature*
> *Stars are nets, and fishes we,*
> *Gods the midnight's fantasy.*

To Khlebnikov the revelation that life works in this way brings some kind of comfort. At least he knows what it all means, and that is something. If men are governed by blind powers, there are no more questions to be asked, and even the war falls into place.

A close but fortuitous parallel to Khlebnikov is Isaac Rosenberg (1890–1918), who fought in the British army and was killed on the western front. Though he was of Russian descent, he cannot have known Khlebnikov's work, and his resemblances must be of temperament or origin. Though, in depicting the actual face of the battlefield, he surpasses in realistic detail all English poets of the war, he sought for some cosmic explanation and was a seer in the sweep of his insight and his interpretation of destruction as the fulfilment of forces at work from the distant past. In 'The Burning of the Temple'[12] he tells how all that the efforts of men have done for centuries to build civilisation has been ruined in a destruction which is like the death of a great

47

king, whose work has lasted for many years. Rosenberg laments the passing of a beautiful and ordered world, and so fearful is this passing that it resembles some appalling reversal in nature, in which the sun forsakes its course and creates universal destruction. He sees the war in a gigantic perspective and is a witness of doom. Yet with all his passion and vision Rosenberg does not completely succeed as a poet. His occasional faultiness in grammar may be due to his foreign origin and need not much disturb us, but it is more disturbing that sometimes we have to read his lines two or three times before we see what rhythm they are intended to have. In him the creative urge is not matched by an equal command of form, and some of his most impressive poems have the air of being drafts for others to come later. Perhaps this gap between conception and achievement is inevitable to war-poets who have to snatch what moments they can from other, tyrannical duties. But the reason may lie deeper than that. We find much the same thing in Wilfred Owen (1893–1918), whose emotions are so strong that they sometimes brush aside refinements of composition as if they were below his notice, and this surely is why Yeats formed so low an opinion of him.[13] These poets were so occupied with their themes that their actual presentation was not of paramount concern. They were indeed caught in a dilemma. On the one hand they could write smoothly and easily in the Georgian idiom, as Sassoon did, and then we complain that they are not facing the full issues before them. On the other hand, in disregard of this inadequate manner, they might experiment with freer and bolder forms without quite knowing to what these would lead them. For them the urgent, immediate task was to transform their troubles into poetry, and in the last resort they had not yet the technique to make the most of their themes. They were after all young men, driven into poetry by their peculiar conditions, and not professional poets who had time to study and evolve new methods. The old prophetic spirit was more at home in stately measures and a sonorous language, but these did not suit actual participation in war, and the break into more modern manners, of which Rosenberg was dimly conscious, was not at his full disposal. The most successful war-poets were those who had no disposition to prophesy and wrote about their personal sensations in brilliant adaptations of the new methods. The war was not well suited to the prophetic manner, but soon enough the world saw other troubles which almost called aloud for it.

If the First World War was the fulfilment of one class of prophecies, the Russian Revolution in 1917 was the start of another, at least in its own country. When it came, Blok believed that at last all his agonies and uncertainties had come to an end and that the whole world had been transformed overnight. In this enthralling mood in January 1918 he wrote Двенадцать (*The Twelve*). His style has changed with his outlook. He uses new rhythms drawn from popular songs and dances, a close, clipped, colloquial language, images of violence and destruction drawn from twelve soldiers on the loot and a girl who has deserted them and whom they kill in a momentary fit of fury. It is an apt myth of the revolutionary scene, set in ice-bound Petrograd where wind and snow blind the eyes. The soldiers have no aim but destruction, no motives but hate and jealousy, and yet Blok suddenly turns from their squabbles and boasts when, to our astonishment, in a style much richer and more melodious than hitherto, he comes to his conclusion:

> ...Так идут державным шагом —
> Позади — голодный пес,
> Впереди — с кровавым флагом,
> И за вьюгой невидим,
> И от пули невредим,
> Нежной поступью надвьюжной,
> Снежной россыпью жемчужной,
> В белом венчике из роз —
> Впереди — Исус Христос.[14]

> ...*On they march with sovereign tread,—*
> *With a starving dog behind,*
> *With a blood-red flag ahead,*
> *Through the storm where none can see,*
> *From the rifle-bullets free,*

*Gently walking on the snow,*
*Where the pearly snow-flakes glow,*
*Marches rose-crowned in the van*
*Jesus Christ, the Son of Man.*

Into *The Twelve*, which was almost his last poem, Blok put his vision of the Revolution, of a Russia liberated and transformed, of desperate hopes at last realised. It is the crown of prophetic poetry in the first quarter of this century, and though the twelve soldiers suggest the twelve Apostles, and though the presence of Christ at the end pulls the poem together and explains what the march of the soldiers through the snowstorm means, it is all the more remarkable because Blok did not believe in Christianity and made no concealment of the fact. When he introduced Christ as the leader of the Revolution, his friends were amazed and asked what he meant. His answer was: 'If you look carefully at the columns of snow on this road you will see Jesus Christ.'[15] He put Christ there because he could not see the Russian people on the march without him, and in this he was entirely true to his vision. If we press the point, this is what despite his unbelief he always took for granted. For him Christ is not the Christ of the Orthodox Church, nor of any theology, but simply the incarnation of the most tender and most generous impulses in the Russian soul. Blok creates his own religion and finds his own symbols for it, and among them is Christ, who is needed as the only possible figure that can give meaning to so tumultuous and so violent a change. Blok, the prophet, sees incalculable forces at work and presents them exactly as he sees them.

Blok makes no forecast of the future beyond indicating a divine leadership towards some undescried goal. For him the Revolution was at this moment so overwhelming that he was totally absorbed by its present reality. But other poets also saw it as a promise of tremendous things to come and, though they treated it in ways very unlike Blok's, they show how deeply it appealed to the Russian desire for some transfiguring apocalypse. The old notion of Holy Russia was given a new life in new forms. Even Nikolai Gumilev (1886–1921), who was opposed to the Revolution and shot for an alleged conspiracy against it, believed in some splendid fate for Russia and not long before his death wrote:

Сердце будет пламенем палимо
Вплоть до дня, когда взойдут, ясны,
Стены Нового Иерусалима
На полях моей родной страны.

И тогда повеет ветер странный —
И прольется с неба страшный свет,
Это Млечный Путь расцвел нежданно
Садом ослепительных планет.[16]

*So my heart will burn and mind condemn,*
*Till the glorious day when there will stand*
*Golden walls of New Jerusalem*
*In the pastures of my native land.*

*Eerie winds will blow and bless the hour,*
*And the skies will send a blinding ray*
*From the planets, stars and suns in flower,*
*In the gardens of the Milky Way.*

Gumilev did not elaborate his dream with any precision, but even after the Revolution he was still confident that a glorious destiny awaited Russia. His belief was only partly religious, or rather its religious aspect was strengthened by his belief in Russia's predestined part in shaping the world. He was true to the old trust that in the end his country would win an un-exampled reward for its long years of suffering, and this reward would be both secular and spiritual.

The same belief was to be held in different forms by men who were in total disagreement with Gumilev on almost every subject. For Andrei Bely the Revolution was in some sense a fulfilment of what he had long dreamed, and his fullest response was a long poem, Христос Воскрес (*Christ is Risen*), which unfortunately falls below his usual brilliance. He sees indeed so powerful a reawakening that it may well be compared to a resurrection, but his visions are too diaphanous to make any real impact. His art is not at its best on this large scale, and he is much more successful when he writes quite a short poem, 'Родине' ('To my Native Land'), in which he sees his country as passing through a destructive conflagration to a celestial glory. He too relies on his own private brand of Christianity and sees angels in the sky and a new glory shining on the world:

Сухие пустыни позора,
Моря неизливные слез —
Лучем безглагольного взора
Согреет сошедший Христос.

Пусть в небе — и кольца Сатурна,
И млечных путей серебро, —
Кипи фосфорически бурно,
Земли огневое ядро![17]

*The dry, barren wastes of dishonour,*
*The seas of unquenchable tears,*
*From light in His look, though he speak not,*
*Will sparkle when Christ's face appears.*

*Leave Heaven its girdle of Saturn,*
*Its milky and silvery ways;*
*And seethe, blaze like light in the tempest,*
*Earth-ball, with thy fiery rays!*

Bely's excitement is different from Blok's. He sees the present disorder not as the prelude to some future splendour but as a sudden illumination which will cancel past faults and failures and in which Christ is not a symbol but himself. Bely's revelation is indeed religious, and though the Bolsheviks left him alone, he spoke not for the new age which they promised but for the old age which they destroyed.

Another kind of apocalypse was foreseen by a generation of poets younger than that of Blok and Bely, who called themselves Futurists, though their Futurism had little in common with the raucous violence of Marinetti except a rather touching belief in machines. Just as the Hebrew prophets varied their prophecies of doom and their denunciations of evil-doing with visions of celestial peace on earth, of Paradises of physical abundance and social justice, so the Futurists, who had from the start been revolutionaries and now found themselves unbelievably released from tsarism and war, indulged in uninhibited flights of fancy. They foresaw a not too distant future when the resources of nature should be so harnessed by man that there would be no hunger or poverty, and men would live at peace with one another throughout the world. Khlebnikov, whose genius had many facets, now turned his eyes to the future and forecast marvellous changes. In his 'Город будущего' ('The City of the Future') he depicts dream cities, which sometimes recall those of Rimbaud's *Les Illuminations*, but more often the scientific romances of H. G. Wells. Khlebnikov delineates the city of the future with a firm, even precise imagination. It is in a single piece made not of stone but of glass, mathematically shaped in rectangles and curves to resemble a huge honeycomb:

> Где только мера и длина,
> Где небо пролито из синего кувшина.[18]

> *Where all is measurement and line,*
> *Where sky is poured from a dark-blue jug.*

Yet this notion, worthy of Corbusier and not absolutely unlike some of the more adventurous achievements of modern architects, has a mysterious, romantic side. The summits of the glass buildings are like hair, and the streets have water-nymphs in them. Nor need we doubt that Khlebnikov means this to be taken more or less literally. He combines his advanced technology with a belief in a return to nature and in the presence of unseen powers which give life to everything. This is the setting of a new society, over which a tranquil priestess presides, while its participants listen to the voice of all humanity and know all the knowledge that is worth knowing. Khlebnikov thought that this dream could be realised, and into it he throws his desire for a refashioned world in which existence is simple and tranquil and knowledge is an open book. It was at some such goal that he thought the Revolution to be aiming, and in 'Ладомир' ('Ladomir') he urged his countrymen to seek a practical version of it. When it comes, men will live in harmony with nature, whose powers will give them peace and strength. Distinctions of race and money and geography will be obliterated, and, as we might expect from Khlebnikov, who was a crank about philology and held fantastic views on the nature of language, there will be a universal speech, which will be a sign of man's unity with nature:

> Всегда, навсегда, там и здесь!
> Всем все, всегда и везде —
> Наш клич пролетит по звезде!
> Язык любви над миром носится
> И Песня Песней в небо просится.[19]
>
> *Ever, for ever, there and here!*
> *For all, always and everywhere!*
> *Up to the stars will rise our cry!*
> *Love's language over the world will fly,*
> *And the Song of Songs be borne to the sky!*

Khlebnikov was, even by Russian standards, a wild eccentric, and his poetry varies in quality because he is not equally obsessed by all the themes which catch his wayward temperament, but in many inspired moments he shares the visionary exaltation which the Revolution evoked in its first years. While Blok presents the crash of a falling world, Khlebnikov looks into the future and sees the fulfilment of reckless but not utterly inconceivable dreams.

For a short time something of the same kind happened to Mayakovsky. As a young man he consoled himself for his sorrows by predicting the Revolution, and was not far wrong when he said that it would come in 1916. He had in him a deep vein of melancholy which he countered partly by self-mockery and partly by his belief that the Revolution would solve all problems personal and political. When it came, he embraced its cause wholeheartedly, and was willing to do anything for it. Though he squandered his talents on many ephemeral activities, for about five years he allowed his genius full play in celebration of the new world which, like Khlebnikov, he thought to be waiting round the corner. His extraordinary lyrical gift, with its combination of wild fancy, exuberant humour, and exultant confidence, enabled him to create a truly revolutionary poetry about the Revolution. Though some of his best pieces are short poems which deal with specific issues and are meant to be actual marching-songs or attacks on the enemies of the Revolution, he was capable of writing on an extended scale, and his *150,000,000*[20] is an epic flight of fantasy, in which a colossal peasant called Ivan, whose arm is as long as the river Neva and whose heels are like the steppes, wades across the Atlantic, where he fights hand to hand with Woodrow Wilson, whose top hat is as tall as the Eiffel Tower. This is largely a boisterous farce, written in the highest of spirits and rich in knock-about fun. But it contains its forecast for the future, which is of course that Russia confounds the United States. In Мистерия-буфф (*Mystery-Bouffe*)[21] Mayakovsky presents a long, lyrical, Aristophanic drama, where his gifts work together in a brilliant unity. In it the earth is destroyed by a deluge, and the few survivors, Clean and Unclean, struggle for mastery. The Unclean win, visit Paradise but reject it as hungry and joyless, then return to earth and by repairing the damage done by the war enter the Promised Land, where machines provide plenty for everyone. The main assumptions are simple enough, but the vitality with which they are worked out is enormous, and at the end Mayakovsky almost convinces us that his Utopia will at least not be boring, so keen is his zest for it and so lively his humour even when he is at his most serious. He certainly deserves to be called a prophet, though we do not usually expect prophets to treat their themes in this ebullient spirit. Despite his complete rejection of orthodox religion, he has an unbounded faith in the future of mankind on the earth and, like modern Russians, he sees human dominion extending beyond it, when in 'Наш Марш' ('Our March') he says:

> Видите, скушно звезд небу!
> Без него наши песни вьем.
> Эй, Большая Медведица! требуй,
> чтоб на небо нас взяли живьем.
>
> Радости пей! Пой!
> В жилах весна разлита.
> Сердце, бей бой!
> Грудь наша — медь литавр.[22]

*See, the stars are too bored to bother!*
*Without them our singing shall blow.*
*Oh, ask, Great Bear, our Mother,*
*That alive to the stars we go.*

*Drink of delight! Sing! Shout!*
*Veins with the spring-flood thrumming.*
*Hearts, up! Strike out!*
*Our breasts are brass cymbals drumming.*

If Mayakovsky's prayer has not yet been fully answered, it is not totally impossible that it will be, and its exultant confidence helps to explain much that has happened in recent years.

This phase of prophetic, Utopian poetry did not last long. If it began in 1917, it ended in 1922, partly from disillusion in the poets themselves, partly from the official policy of turning poets to write on immediately profitable tasks. But in its five years this poetry did something almost unprecedented in European literature. Its ebullience was no doubt largely due to the release of forces that had for long been kept silent, and that is why it takes so lively a form. But prophetic poetry is not usually like this, and only very uncommon conditions are likely to produce it. In its older and graver form it continued to perform its special task in the hands of at least one man of genius. At the other end of Europe from Russia, a poet, whose gifts in some ways resembled Blok's but who was as far as possible from sharing his ideas of revolution, was to turn the prophetic spirit to no less formidable problems, to the state of the world and of western civilisation between one war and the next. Yeats was always and essentially an Irishman, who allowed himself the privilege to be at times extremely harsh about Ireland. From it he drew his myths and symbols, his sense of mysteries behind the visible scene, his sharp, puncturing criticism, his magnificent manner, his sense of personalities and of their place in history. In a sense he always wrote about Ireland, from his first dream-laden verse about figures of Celtic mythology to 'The Black Tower', which he composed within a week of his death. Yet though Ireland was the source and the focus of his inspiration, he found so much in it and felt so strongly about what he found, that in his hands it became a microcosm of the whole civilised world. Its troubles were the troubles of Europe; its civilisation, seen through his admiration and his anxieties, was infinitely precious because it was derived from a long tradition of humanity and humanism. Yeats was forced, almost in spite of himself, to write about public matters. Through his first controversies to his noble and deeply serious poems on the Rebellion of 1916, he found himself driven into the arena of public affairs and had to form means to deal with them.

Yeats's direction was settled when he began to work on the theories which in 1926 he was to embody in *A Vision*, and owed largely to the discovery that his wife had mediumistic powers. Yeats, like Blok, had always been in a peculiar and unorthodox way a religious man. On abandoning the faith of his fathers he sought another to take its place and found it by combining elements which had long played a part in occult thought and won some favour in his youth. Like Blok, he relied not on science and proof, but on insight and inspired intuition, but he was too critical to take inspiration just as it came, and found satisfaction in constructing a system of cycles partly from what he learned from spirits, partly from his own interpretation of history. He treated this with entire seriousness, and in any assessment of him it must be recognised as fundamental to his mature outlook and responsible for much of his finest work. It is often present in his poetry, and, if sometimes we are barely conscious of it, that is not because Yeats wishes to play it down but because he believes that a poet should not admit argument and disputation into his work. His theories provide a background and a foundation for his poetry on public affairs, and it gains much of its splendour from them. However much he owed to his sharp insight into current affairs, he saw his subjects as related to a scheme of things which was very much his own invention and yet with a little trouble perfectly intelligible to his readers. Thus his magnificent poem 'The Second Coming'[23] is indeed a forecast of undeciphered evils and forces us to respond to its astonishing power, but it fits easily into Yeats's theory of historical cycles and owes some of its assurance to them. His intellectual understanding and his emotional drive are perfectly fused, and each gains much from the other. Yeats is a prophet not merely because he prophesies what is to come but because he sees human life from an exalted standpoint and passes from the immediate issue which engages him to wider and more disturbing considerations. Like most prophets, he prophesies evil things. He has no belief in Utopias and speaks with pitying contempt of those who work for them, as he does of Eva Gore-Booth in the poem written in memory of her and of her sister, Con Markiewicz:

> I know not what the younger dreams—
> Some vague Utopia—and she seems,
> When withered old and skeleton-gaunt,
> An image of such politics.[24]

For Yeats such events as the Russian Revolution or the Irish Civil War are merely confirmatory evidence that the world has taken a sharp turn for the worse, that the abandonment of old habits is a prelude to bloodshed and lawlessness, that our old optimism has been discredited, and that our whole human condition has become a battle against triumphant evils. Yeats's interest in politics goes back to before the war when he wrote with passion about the hostile reception given to Synge's *Playboy of the Western World* and the obtuse Philistinism of the Municipal Corporation of Dublin in the matter of Hugh Lane's pictures. There perhaps he might seem to make too much of his subject by appealing to the Italian Renaissance or to the men of '98, but now he has found his full scope and his subjects are worthy of the passion and the eloquence which he spends on them. His indignation at the collapse not only of courtesy and chivalry but of common respect for life stings him into an authority which is comparable to Dante's denunciations of his own Florence or of the kings and popes who have ruined Italy.

At the end of his life Yeats wrote 'The Black Tower', and though he speaks in less commanding tones than in his prime, and though it is not so much a summary as a conclusion of his life's work, it shows with a power astonishing in an old man his last judgement on a world at war with itself and marked by the decay and dishonour into which many noble things have fallen. The poem moves on two levels—in the main stanzas, which speak of the tower in its loyal defence of what might be thought a lost cause, and in the slightly varied refrains which hint at a supernatural background and give a new dimension to the situation. The tower, which has long been a symbol in Yeats's poetry, may stand for Ireland or Europe or a whole system of life, and is surely all three, but it enshrines an unfailing loyalty to some ancient cause or tradition, and presents Yeats's view of the civilised life. The guardians of the tower are poor, but they are faithful, even though they are approached with bribes and worldly arguments of expediency. Among them is a man whose vision passes beyond theirs, and though his companions do not believe him, they remain true to their trust. Behind them are the dead in a tomb. These incarnate the past which is half forgotten, and watch the present in fear of what may happen, giving their invisible support to those who still believe in them:

> There in the tomb the dark grows blacker,
> But wind comes up from the shore:
> They shake when the winds roar,
> Old bones upon the mountain shake.[25]

At the end of his life Yeats, seeing many of his prophecies fulfilled, placed his trust in the strength of the past to keep men true by exerting its spiritual power from beyond the grave. For him civilisation was a living force in the souls of men. This poem was written in January 1939, and before the end of the year, after Yeats's death, the world was again to be convulsed in slaughter and destruction. 'The Black Tower' marks the end of an epoch, which had indeed kept much that was worth keeping from the past and was threatened with incalculable changes. The struggle which he depicted in this enigmatic form could be interpreted in many ways, but in all of them what counts is the conviction that human dignity is in danger and can be saved only by being true to itself.

In Yeats and Blok the prophetic spirit sets formidable powers to work and inspires poetry which by its most uncommon grasp rises to the huge challenges that face it. Despite its forecasts of disaster it is moved by so lofty a confidence and so dominating a vision that it rides over minor considerations and advances undeterred by hesitations and afterthoughts to its mysterious goal. Its temper runs counter to the precise, analytical poetry which began to show itself about 1910 and is most at home in self-examination and the fine discriminations which the prophets brush aside in their concentration on a single end. It inevitably lacks their onslaught and vigour and ability to take in the whole universe in a single sweeping survey or to pass judgements with unquestioning authority. Yet there are times when we might think that it too has something prophetic in it, notably when it analyses the spiritual troubles of our time. When T. S. Eliot (1889–1965) wrote *The Waste Land*, his subject was the sickness of modern urban, or suburban, middle-class life, and he diagnosed with clinical insight what this sickness is and how it works. He was to this degree a seer, and the last lines of the poem might almost entitle him to be called a prophet. A subject so intimate and so disturbing justifies a prophetic approach, but we miss that supernatural element which is essential to prophetic poetry. Eliot points with unerring precision to what is wrong, but he is not guided by any religious vision, and when in his later works he is so guided, they cease to be prophetic and belong to poetry concerned with the struggles and the shortcomings of the human soul. Nor even in *The Waste Land* does he look on the state of the world as such. The convulsive climax with which it ends is not for the world but for the individual, something that may happen to anyone but not to society as a whole. Eliot's poetry is exclusively personal, even though it is painfully relevant to a large number of persons.

Yet despite this powerful impulse to write the poetry of the inner self outside temporary limitations, the need for prophetic poetry was still felt in times of hideous urgency, and once or twice before the Second World War it took a modified but still powerful form. It might be attached to Christian myth and imagery, as David Gascoyne (b. 1916) used it in his long and finely sustained 'Miserere'[26] to illuminate the agony of the persecuted and the downtrodden. His poem has an immediate reference to the present state of the world, to the tyranny of power over the innocent, and though his Christ is the Christ of Christianity, he has much that Blok would have understood, and embodies forces which must in the end conquer because they are the strongest in the human soul. Gascoyne prophesies not doom but deliverance, and his strength lies more in his denunciation of evils than in his forecast of their disappearance. He lacks the tremendous sweep of Blok or Yeats, and this not merely from a difference of talent but because he speaks in more conventional terms and evokes less astonishment and surprise. The conditions which drove an elder generation to prophesy with such confidence had less hold on Gascoyne, and he shows how the prophetic manner loses some of its majesty when it gives up its independence and special authority.

A variation on the prophetic spirit can be seen in some poems of the Spanish Civil War, which inspired much poetry of many kinds, and though this is not among the most prominent, it has its own distinction. One or two poets get away from immediate issues and in their attempt to form a picture of the tragic destiny of Spain not only pass beyond the present but turn to prophetic fury in their anger and indignation. So León Felipe, deeply troubled by the divisions which rend his country, finds in the axe an image for them and denounces the hideous spirit which always drives his countrymen. His manner is modernistic, but nothing obstructs the direct assault of his agonised condemnation:

> Tú y yo y España
> no somos más que polvo.
> Polvo,
> polvo,
> polvo...
> Nuestra es el hacha,

el hacha y el desierto...
el desierto amarillo
donde descansa el hacha
cuando no quede ya
ni una raíz
ni un recuerdo
ni un hombre.[27]

*You and I and Spain*
*are no more than dust.*
*Dust,*
*dust,*
*dust...*
*Ours is the axe,*
*the axe and the desert,*
*the yellow desert*
*where the axe finds rest,*
*when already there remains*
*neither a root*
*nor a memory*
*nor a man.*

Felipe universalises his horror and has the true prophetic touch in the sweep and violence of his indignation. He is not strictly a prophetic poet, since he does not forecast, but he is at least a seer who in the present state of Spain sees its unchanging nature, and he has learned something from the prophetic manner, even though he applies to it a new technique.

This kind of horrified indignation is a driving power also in Luis Cernuda (1904–63) at the same time. Prophetic grandeur is no more common with him than with most Spaniards, but sometimes he is so outraged that, like Felipe, he denounces his country for a brutality which nothing can abate. He moves beyond his usual harsh words for Spain and allows his vision a wider sweep, as in 'A un poeta muerto' ('To a dead poet'), which he wrote on the death of Federico García Lorca. In it he looks from the present to the past and the future and sees no prospect of anything but hate and destruction for Spain. He is moved by the misery of an irreparable personal loss, and in his grief for his murdered friend he denounces his country for its cruelty and hatred. For him Lorca was killed because he was a mainspring of life and light, such as his countrymen have always hated in their hearts, and it is this which drives him into bitter condemnation:

> El odio y destrucción perduran siempre
> sordamente en la entraña
> toda hiel sempiterna del español terrible,
> que acecha lo cimero
> con su piedra en la mano.[28]

> *Hate and destruction always last*
> *secretly in the bowels*
> *all the everlasting gall of the terrible Spaniard,*
> *who lies in ambush for the summit*
> *with his stone in his hand.*

Like Felipe, Cernuda universalises a single experience and draws his ghastly lesson from it. He resembles prophet-poets in the wide sweep of his perception and in the authority with which he judges his country. This condemnation, which amounts to hatred, is the reverse side of the love which Spaniards feel for their country, and fundamentally not very unlike it. They are so concerned with Spain, so convinced that they are part of it, that they watch its behaviour with an agonised attention and feel as personal injuries its faults and crimes. Even now a younger generation, which never knew the Civil War, still feels that its country has a tragic destiny and observes its actions with watchful fear, passing easily beyond the present moment to a sense of timeless destiny.[29] This is an aftermath of the prophetic spirit more than a survival from it, and it marks the transition to a different kind of poetry, in which the personal element is much more to the fore and the poet does not take so embracing a view of his subject. But it is from prophetic poetry that Cernuda derives his inexorable authority, his breadth and scope and fury.

In sharp contrast with these Spanish poets and their harsh or despairing judgements on their country stands an Englishman who had absorbed much of their outlook and shared their sorrows but came to a different conclusion. George Barker

(b. 1913) felt to the full the horrors of the Spanish Civil War and wrote about them with a rich scope of prophetic grandeur and mystery. His English antecedents made it easier for him to approach such a theme than his Spanish contemporaries could with their Mediterranean liking for clear issues and their distrust of any mystical leanings unless they are rooted in the Catholic Church. In 'Elegy for Spain' Barker sees in present events signs and symbols of much vaster issues and knows that the sight of a dead child reveals abysses of depravity and horror. His basic conception is that Spain is being martyred by evil men, by Mussolini and Hitler and their Spanish allies, and this martyrdom is not for any religious cause but simply for liberty. Those who defend it with their lives are martyrs in the truest sense of the word, and to them he offers the same consolations as have always been paid to martyrs for any noble cause. Just as the flowers still blossom and the birds still sing in the midst of war, so the human desire for freedom still lives and is kept alive by the blood of those who fight for it. In the end their cause will triumph:

> Those who die with five stars in their hand,
> Hand on their ghosts to guard a yard of land
> From the boot of the landlord and the band of war.[30]

This conclusion emerges from a series of powerful images chosen to convey the elements of life and death in the war. Barker sees Spain as a noble bull brutally done to death, but at the same time he evokes the strange Spanish sense of blood as the very stuff of life, which, even when it is spilled, somehow restores and revivifies. Yet, though he speaks for Spaniards in their own imagery, his prophetic quality comes not from them but from the north with its brooding sense of mystery and its sudden flashes of insight into the distant, almost impenetrable darkness.

A sequence of convulsions on a large scale turned the eyes of prophet-poets from the future to the present, but this does not mean that there was no longer any need for them. The present can be seen in its relation to eternity and contains the seeds of destinies to come. What counts is the spacious vision, the gift to see beyond immediate issues to what lies behind them, the sense of cosmic urgency in the doings of men. It is this which became the driving force in Edith Sitwell (1888–1964). In *Gold Coast Customs* she applied her finely wrought, sensitive art to a subject of huge scope and presented her disgust at the emptiness and brutality of much modern life. Writing in 1929 she saw the barbarism below the surface and foretold that it could end only in destruction. To this degree the Second World War proved her right, and in it she applied her gifts with a new tautness to the pathos and misery of the moment. When she deals with the first air-raids on London, she sees them as examples of a far wider and deeper distress, and though she knows what it means for lovers to be separated, she feels a special grief at the prospect of inevitable separation by death. Her tender compassion sometimes finds an outlet in biting irony which adds to the poignancy of the human scenes which she imagines. So in 'Serenade: Any Man to Any Woman' she turns a famous theme upside down and makes it much more distressing and more suited to the dark occasion:

> And so I love you till I die—
> (Unfaithful I, the cannon's mate):
> Forgive my love of such brief span,
> But fickle is the flesh of man,
> And death's cold puts the passion out.[31]

What she grasps is the universal situation behind many particular instances, but she gives to it the intensity and intimacy of a personal attitude. The strict form controls her powerful emotions, and the epigrammatic neatness increases the horror. The prophetic note may have lost some of its scope, but it is abundantly present in the authority and decisiveness of her utterance.

At 8.15 a.m., 6 August 1945, the first atomic bomb was dropped on Hiroshima, and this so appalled and horrified Edith Sitwell that it changed the direction of her poetry. On the actual event she wrote three poems, 'Dirge for the New Sunrise', 'The Shadow of Cain', and 'The Canticle of the Rose'. For her the bomb was more horrifying even than the war. The neat shape of her war-poems gives place to much freer forms, longer lines, more varied rhythms, and more internal assonance and rhyme; the chaos of the actual situation which now obsesses her drives her to a more complex treatment and a more comprehensive vision, and in this she loses something in tension and singleness of aim. But the prophetic note sounds with force as she looks into the future and asks what retribution will come to man for tearing open the bowels of the earth and destroying the very principle of life. She attacks her task at various levels, and her imagery reflects her gradations and changes of feeling. On one side she is moved by her profound compassion for man in the hideous disorder of his own making, and in particular she sees him as reduced to his primal elements, the bone of his body and the spark of his spirit. On the other side she denounces the theorists who believe that their experiments, conducted with so wanton an expenditure of life, will create a new civilisation and improve the condition of mankind. This she most emphatically rejects, seeing in such claims 'the sound too high for our hearing' and identifying them with the highest mathematical idea, which is zero.[32] Edith Sitwell displays her inexpressible horror at the results to which uncontrolled discovery may lead, and against them she sets the pitiful rights of humanity. Her attitude recalls in some ways that of Heym and Trakl before 1914, but the compassion which inspires and drives her is not only more fully at work than theirs, but related, as theirs was not, to a Christian faith, and that is why she foresees with such immediacy a Judgement Day when Christ will reappear and cleanse the world. Her Christian figures fit into her cosmic visions and make them more intelligible. Yet, though she belongs to a truly English tradition of poetry, she is a solitary figure in the last twenty years, speaking for a unity of outlook which belongs to a more spacious age than our own.

Today prophetic poetry is very rare, and though we can suggest more than one reason for this, perhaps the most fundamental is that it is essentially a religious art which no longer appeals to the modern spirit. It is not necessarily tied to any creed, and is often wilful and solitary in choosing the tenets of its faith, but it remains religious in its sense of supernatural powers at work in the world, controlling and enriching it but above it and apart from it. They belong to a higher order to which the poet has access and from which he draws his knowledge and his power. Prophetic poetry rejects the scientific spirit as alien to imaginative creation and finds a substitute in inspired insight. It would be idle to pretend that most modern poets know much about science or are actively interested in it, but their outlooks and presuppositions cannot fail to be deeply affected by it. They have been brought up to accept its account of the visible world, to believe that the senses are the source of knowledge, to see events as parts of an implacable causal system, and to suspect attempts to explain them otherwise, except sometimes on very orthodox religious lines. To younger poets mystical or metaphysical assumptions on any large scale are unwelcome because they claim too much and are incapable of verification. It is safer and often more honest to keep clear of them and to confine onself to what is known. Nor indeed has prophetic poetry been common in history. In many centuries it has played no part, and its sudden, splendid emergence in the first part of this century is perhaps due to a special situation in which Darwinism and the historical spirit had undermined much established belief but many people needed something to take its place and found it in synthetic creeds of their own making, which cannot be expected to win many converts and usually die with their authors. For a few years this spirit inspired a few magnificently gifted poets, but they could not produce disciples comparable to themselves, and after them poetry moved in a new direction in accord with the demands of a less confident and less mystical age.

The decline of the prophetic attitude has meant a withdrawal from the wider horizons of the imagination, and in this we may see a diminution of power and grandeur. We no longer feel ourselves actors in some cosmic drama or ennobled by the transcendental seriousness of the issues which we have to face and the circumstances in which we face them. We miss the conviction and the majesty with which Blok and Yeats treated the human predicament, and to this extent we may feel that poetry has lost something in ultimate urgency and that nothing is as wonderful as we once thought. Yet this is not the right diagnosis. Things are just as serious as they always were, but we look at them differently and explain them by other means. We may find ourselves encompassed by a darkness which we cannot pierce, but that is no reason why we should not have a positive policy for it. In the end this means that we must dispense with forecasts and promises and accept the moment as it is, and this is the spirit which seems now to be emerging and has very recently received noble expression from Dagmar Nick (b. 1926), who in 'Mene Mene Tekel' explicitly quotes a text which conveys the very breath of prophecy, and calls upon us to take no notice of it. Her opening lines state her position with decisive clarity:

> Nimm diese Botschaft nicht an.
> Der gezeichnete Himmel
> besagt nichts.
> Unbeirrt finden die Stare heim
> durch die tödliche Schrift.
> Auch die Donner
> im purpurnen Wind der Frühe
> sind ohne Belang.
> Den liebenden stürzte schon immer
> der Boden unter dem Herzen.

> *Do not accept this message.*
> *The signs on the sky*
> *say nothing.*
> *Unerringly the starlings find their way*
> *home through the deadly writing.*
> *Even the thunderclaps*
> *in the purple wind of the dawn*
> *are without consequence.*
> *From under lovers' hearts*
> *the ground has always fallen away.*

Dagmar Nick insists that we must pay no attention to signs and portents since they mean nothing. What counts is that life continues, for good or ill, in spite of them, and this is what concerns us. She goes on to say that things are always mixed and that examples of life and destruction flourish together everywhere, and from this she draws her conclusion:

Sieh nicht hin:
überspringe die Angst.[33]

*Do not look:*
*jump over your fear.*

Dagmar Nick speaks for a generation which distrusts attempts to peer into the unknown and believes that a critical approach to reality is better than even the most inspired guess. In her view the mystery of life lies not in inscrutable powers around it but in what we see and do here and now, and towards this she is entirely constructive. The old distances have receded out of sight, and we must look at the present moment and refuse to be dispirited by its menaces. This is not an ignoble conclusion, and it offers poets many opportunities to display their gifts in mastering the issues which confront them.

## CHAPTER 3

# THE PRIVATE VISION

In the last forty years poetry has steadily moved from conscious majesty and a cosmic outlook to the careful presentation of private sensations and states of mind. In this it has had a counterpart in philosophy, which with equal determination has moved from the construction of vast systems in the Hegelian manner to the close examination of words as they are actually used. Both these changes are from synthesis to analysis, and poetry and philosophy have alike turned the tables on themselves by finding their main activity in what used to be a mere part of their technique. If philosophy has been influenced by the empirical methods of modern science, poetry has been deeply affected by brutal reality. It has discovered that it can no longer accept many assumptions that it believed to be true and that it cannot take a matter for granted just because it wishes to. In it the transformation has been from a desire to be comfortably universal to a conviction that only through a very precise attention to particulars can it be anything at all. It seeks particularity not merely in the concrete presentation of a theme but in the nature of the theme itself. Instead of moving outwards in pursuit of unfamiliar universes, it moves inward to unexamined recesses of the self. In the end it may find something universal, but this is not to be sought as such in the first instance. For this change a price has to be paid. Poetry has become shy of its old breadth and seldom attempts it. It may even have lost some of its energy and confidence, since the poet who dissects his feelings with an intimate curiosity may become earthbound and miss the chance of flight on some brilliant spontaneity. The change is extremely relevant to the whole question of political poetry. If we no longer look for the wide scope and exalted understanding of the prophetic poets, we look for more poignant and more revealing qualities, for the illumination which comes from something clearly seen in all its complexity and presented, despite its novelty, in a way which cannot fail to engage us and make us feel at home with it.

At the start it is surprising that poets who probe their own hidden corners should be interested in public affairs at all or find in them subjects for their art. These must surely be too crude, too disorderly, too unmanageable for so sensitive an approach and demand too violent an adjustment for the poet to admit them to his privacy. Poets who have spent their lives perfecting their acquaintance with themselves are not likely to respond to the loud claims of political affairs or to find that their creative powers are set to work by them. And in fact this is often the case. Though in the older generation Yeats faced politics with a magnificent confidence, his junior T. S. Eliot was much less ready to do so. What engages his passionate consideration is the corrupt state of man, and this he sees as a universal problem of which everyone should be conscious in himself. That is why he can treat it on a broad scale and yet keep it extremely intimate and particular. Some persistent aspects of public life are relevant to such an outlook, and in 'Triumphal March' and 'Difficulties of a Statesman' Eliot chose as his theme the hard, indifferent, soulless nature of power. The long list of armaments in the first poem and the crazy complexities of administrative detail in the second indicate how remote such activities are from ordinary human nature, still more from the rare moments when it is redeemed by a divine calm. Eliot's symbol for this impersonal, inhuman spirit is that of the military or political leader:

Look

    There he is now, look:
    There is no interrogation in his eyes
    Or in the hands, quiet over the horse's neck,
    And in the eyes watchful, waiting, perceiving, indifferent.[1]

The type is familiar enough, but Eliot passed beyond any individual incarnation of it to its essential nature. He extracted from politics this chilling, remote image and moved in a dimension where nothing matters but the human soul. Though he was deeply concerned with his age, he was not as a poet concerned with particular events in it.

In the Second World War Eliot published in 1942 a piece in verse which he called 'A Note on War Poetry'. He himself classed it among 'occasional verses' and clearly did not claim any special regard for it, but it is written with thoughtful precision, and its quiet movement accords with its serious, explanatory intention. His point is that poetry is a life, and he goes on to say:

> War is not a life: it is a situation,
> One which may neither be ignored nor accepted,
> A problem to be met with ambush and stratagem,
> Enveloped or scattered.

> The enduring is not a substitute for the transient,
> Neither one for the other. But the abstract conception
> Of private experience at its greatest intensity
> Becoming universal, which we call 'poetry',
> May be affirmed in verse.[2]

For Eliot the immediate, practical problems of war are alien to the sustained way of life which is poetry, and call for quite a different response, for action and not for words. War is at once too immediate to pass into any universal treatment and too public to become truly part of ourselves. This explains his imperviousness to it and his inability to write about it. Its infinite particulars have for him no ulterior significance and do not stir him to that intensity which is indispensable to true poetry. This is of course a personal statement, and Eliot does not claim that it is true of all poets or that it ought to be, for there are clearly some for whom the transient phenomena of war can become enduring elements in themselves and their art. But he says what he believes, and in this respect he is a true child of an age which insists on the purity of poetry and its freedom from all falsifying or enfeebling influences from without. In this he speaks also for generations younger than his own, and though some poets in them have written on public affairs, they find it hard to approach them in all their depth and breadth. Before they can be absorbed, the poet must adjust his finely trained sensibility to them, and this is no easy task.

Eliot's attitude on this matter is essentially European, derived from French poets who sought to keep poetry as 'pure' as possible and relegated general themes to the forbidden realm of the impure. It was certainly shared by the two most eminent Spanish poets of the generation just before his. Antonio Machado (1875–1939) and Juan Ramón Jiménez (1881–1958) were both on the Republican side in the Civil War and suffered grievously from it, but neither of them wrote poetry about it.[3] Machado indeed wrote freely in prose about various issues, but at a time when many Spanish poets felt driven to lament the agony of their country, both he and Jiménez were silent. It was not a question of turning their eyes away from the tragic scene or retiring into some remote fastness of art; it was rather that they had so fine a sense of what really touched them that they could not and would not deal with anything else, and the Civil War was too vast and too shapeless a theme for their disciplined sensibilities. Yet, when something happened in it which struck them in their own being as a purely personal issue, they responded fully and nobly to it. When Lorca was shot by the Nationalists in the summer of 1936 at Granada, Machado and Jiménez, both of whom knew and loved him, wrote about his death. Machado's appalled shock finds release in a very restrained and almost factual account of the execution. This is characteristic of his austere art in its self-control and its apt choice of only the most significant details, but it also conveys how commonplace so vile an action looks when it happens, and this keeps the poem at a purely personal level. This is preliminary to another theme which touches Machado very deeply and provides him with his climax. The crime was committed in Granada, which was Lorca's home and had often been celebrated by him:

> ...Que fué en Granada el crimen
> sabed — ¡pobre Granada! — , en su Granada.[4]
>
> *...Know that the crime was in Granada!*
> *Poor Granada! in his Granada.*

For Machado this is a horrifying act of treachery, ingratitude, and unnatural savagery. With his strong Spanish sense of the ties between a man and his birthplace he feels that this is the crowning horror. He makes his point nobly and tragically, but it is very much his own point. Other poets, like Cernuda, might tell what Lorca's murder meant for Spain and for the whole world, but for Machado what counts is its brutal profanation of natural affections. His own inner life has been stricken by this foul action, and he cannot but treat it as a deep personal wound.

On the same occasion Jiménez also wrote a poem, not in the least like Machado's, but at least as personal and intimate and unwilling to enter into any political argument. It is called 'Generalife'[5] and is addressed to Lorca's sister, Isabel. It is a poem about grief, about the overpowering and ultimately cleansing power of tears. This theme it develops with an abundance of imagery and with that hold on diaphanous moods at which Jiménez excels. Having introduced his theme Jiménez gives only one short hint of what has inspired it, a factual reference to the killing of Lorca, whose name is not mentioned. Jiménez, who usually writes about the more delicate states of sensibility in visual or emotional matters, does exactly the same here. The murder of Lorca raises the whole question of grief, and this is his theme. The poem is indeed an act of consolation to the dead man's sister, but in its own right it falls easily into Jiménez's kind of poetry, which is not meant for public affairs and steadfastly eschews them. This is as far as this kind of poet can be expected to go. In the First World War poets like Paul Valéry did not go even so far as this, and never wrote about anything connected with the war. It was from this restricting conception that poets slowly freed themselves, and their escape is even now not complete. The inner sanctuary of the creative self has to be preserved from desecrating intrusions, and public affairs may enter it only if they enrich it and keep it to its unique task.

In 'A Note on War Poetry' Eliot makes two points, the first

explicitly, the second implicitly. He insists that poetry is a life and has nothing to do with matters which are essentially recalcitrant or hostile to it, but at the same time he suggests that among such matters war necessarily has a place. But some poets who would by conviction and temperament share Eliot's view sufficiently to resist saying anything about war are so caught in it that they have to say something, and this is not anything large and embracing but notably particular and private and personal, their own insight into some small part of a vast event which reaches far beyond their own consciousness. In such poetry the poet insists on maintaining at all costs his own integrity and admits only themes which so force themselves on him that he cannot reject them, though even then he deals only with what concerns himself without attempting to survey any wider horizon. So in the First World War Giuseppe Ungaretti (b. 1888), finding himself faced by the prospect of death which faces every soldier, writes a very short, distilled poem, in which, in strict accordance with his practice, every word carries its full weight, and the poem in its small compass makes its point with power and pathos:

Morire come le allodole assetate
sul miraggio

O come la quaglia
passato il mare
nei primi cespugli
perché di volare
non ha piú voglia

Ma non vivere di lamento
come un cardellino accecato[6]

*To die like larks stricken with thirst*
*at the mirage*

*Or like the quail*
*when the sea is passed*
*in the first bushes*
*because it has*
*no more desire to fly*

*But not to live on lamentations*
*like a blinded finch.*

Ungaretti does not mention the war which is directly responsible for turning his thoughts to death, and says nothing about
the conditions in which he writes. He has reduced his poem to
the account of a state of mind, ruthlessly simplified and yet
greatly enriched by the precise, illuminating images. In such
an art we may press every point. Ungaretti considers two forms
of death, both of them appropriate to war. He can either die in
a mirage, as many young men died still believing in some
exalting cause, or he can die because he has lost all wish to live,
and that too is suitable enough for soldiers worn out by effort
and come, as it were, to the end of a long journey. Either of
these he is prepared to accept with resignation, quiet and un-
perturbed. But what he fears and abhors is to live in misery
because of some irreparable loss or mutilation. This is always a
real possibility, and Ungaretti knows what it means. His image
of the blinded finch stands for many kinds of such loss, of
which the very uncertainty makes it more horrible. The alternatives of life and death in war are put forward in their naked
cruelty, and, though such an issue can arise in other situations,
war imposes it inexorably and forces Ungaretti to a decision.
Despite the particular form in which the theme is presented, its
universal significance is manifest and emerges through its
reduction to primal elements.

With this poem of the First World War we may compare
another from the Second. Sidney Keyes (1922–43), who died
in North Africa soon before his twenty-first birthday, had
learned about the death-wish from German poets but did not
himself indulge in it. His forecast of death was a rational
calculation, and he wrote about it with an almost Stoical
detachment:

The red rock wilderness
Shall be my dwelling-place.

Where the wind saws at the bluffs
And the pebble falls like thunder
I shall watch the clawed sun
Tear the rocks asunder.

The seven-branched cactus
Will never sweat wine:
My own bleeding feet
Shall furnish the sign.

The rock says 'Endure'.
The wind says 'Pursue'.
The sun says 'I will suck your bones
And afterwards bury you.'[7]

Keyes courageously examines his position in the harsh, inhuman desert and knows that he is its victim and that its natural elements have him at their mercy. He is able to speak with this detachment because his creative self is safe in its own stronghold of poetry. Just because he insists on his private life, he can face what is coming to him. If we compare his lines with Ungaretti's, we note that the fundamental theme is very much the same, that both poets are concerned with death and do not mention war. But Keyes's poem is much more dependent upon its immediate surroundings than Ungaretti's. He speaks of the desert with a keen eye for its merciless inhumanity and knows that, while it summons him to endurance and initiative, it also threatens him with death. This death is of an unusual, horrifying kind as suits the desert which inflicts it, but Keyes is concerned not with death as such but with his own immediate predicament, its challenges and threats. In this respect, writing some twenty-five years after Ungaretti, he illustrates how in the interval poetry even on the most familiar subjects has become more personal and more particular. Yet, like Ungaretti, Keyes extracts from his particular situation something universal, a complex state of mind which is indeed shaped by the desert but has a relevance far beyond it. His poem is in no sense a departure from his inner poetical life. It arises directly from it, so well has he absorbed his experience and mastered it in himself.

This distillation of an essential poetry from transitory occasions gains by the omission of any reference to the actual shape of the occasions themselves. Elizabeth Langgässer (1899–1950) wrote 'Frühling 1946' ('Spring 1946') about her reunion with her daughter who had been released from the concentration-camp at Auschwitz. She says nothing directly about what has happened but turns it into a myth. The daughter's deliverance comes in the spring, and the joy which it brings to her mother is of light and beauty to someone who has lived in darkness and fear. The myth is built of Greek elements but not actually taken from Greek mythology. Langgässer recalls her anguish and agony during her daughter's absence, and tells what her deliverance means. She sees herself as rising from the toad's dominion, but under her eyelids there is still the redness of Pluto, the god of death, and there still sounds in her ears the hideous pipe played by the guide of the dead. She has seen the gleam in the Gorgon's eye and heard its venom whisper that it can kill her. Against this loathsome background she presents her daughter first as an anemone, then as Nausicaa. The first image catches her springlike freshness, the second the moment of passing from girlhood into womanhood. She has escaped from Styx and Lethe, from death and oblivion, and it is a miracle that she is alive:

> Ohne zu verführen,
> Lebst und bist du da,
> Still mein Herz zu rühren,
> Ohne es zu schüren—
> Kind Nausicaa![8]

> *In you death has no part;*
> *Here, and alive, you are,*
> *Softly to touch my heart,*
> *Nor stir its flames to start,*
> *My child Nausicaa!*

Behind this lies an illimitable wrong, the brutal incarceration of thousands of innocent people, but of this Langgässer says nothing. For her all that matters is the miraculous moment of finding her daughter when she thought that she had lost her, and from her own brilliantly illuminated angle she catches a thrill of transcendent joy in a vast complex of injustice and suffering. It is her hour and her triumph, and her little myth, with its touches of Greek simplicity and sweetness, is entirely apt for her need and conveys the natural purity of her feelings. It marks the unique occasion, the restoration of something infinitely precious which seemed to have been lost beyond hope of recovery, and the escape at last from hideous fears.

Yet even when a poet finds himself driven to write about public affairs, he has still to decide how to do so. Sometimes the relics of his training almost forbid him to do so directly, and he resorts to a somewhat devious method which keeps his artistic conscience intact and throws an oblique light on his contemporary subject. Though Constantine Cavafy takes the Hellenistic and Byzantine past to illustrate many aspects of political and social life, they hardly ever have any reference to a particular modern situation, but are illuminating for their general view of human behaviour in its paradoxes and contradictions. But once he certainly used the past with reference to the present. In the summer of 1922 the Greek armies in Asia Minor were driven to the sea by Mustafa Kemal, and their rout culminated in the bloodthirsty sack of Smyrna. This was the end of Greek ambitions to recover ancient lands in Asia Minor, and an appalling wound to national pride. Cavafy, living in Alexandria, was deeply moved by it, but his response was neither direct nor obvious. It was a short poem called Ὑπὲρ τῆς Ἀχαϊκῆς Συμπολιτείας πολεμήσαντες ('For those who fought for the Achaean League'), and it carries an epigraph saying that it was written by an Achaean in Alexandria in the seventh year of Ptolemy Lathyros, that is 101 B.C. The epigraph places the poet at some distance both in time and place from the actual events and stresses the gap which Cavafy, himself an Alexandrian, feels to exist between himself and Greeks of the mainland. To this anonymous and imaginary character he attributes six straightforward and factual lines:

> Ἀνδρεῖοι σεῖς ποὺ πολεμήσατε καὶ πέσατ' εὐκλεῶς·
> τοὺς πανταχοῦ νικήσαντας μὴ φοβηθέντες.
> Ἄμωμοι σεῖς, ἂν ἔπταισαν ὁ Δίαιος κι ὁ Κριτόλαος.
> Ὅταν θὰ θέλουν οἱ Ἕλληνες να καυχηθοῦν,
> 'Τέτοιους βγάζει τὸ ἔθνος μας' θὰ λένε
> γιὰ σᾶς. Ἔτσι θαυμάσιος θἆναι ὁ ἔπαινός σας.[9]

*You were brave men who fought and fell gloriously;*
*Unafraid of those who had conquered everywhere.*
*You are not to blame, if Diaios and Kritolaos failed.*
*Whenever the Greeks shall be minded to boast,*
*' Our people breeds men like these', they shall say*
*Of you. So marvellous shall be your praise.*

Cavafy sets his epitaph in the decline of the free Greek world
when the Achaean League was twice defeated disastrously by
the Romans in 146 B.C. On the first occasion it was led by
Diaios and on the second by Kritolaos, and both were held
responsible for what happened.[10] This was precisely the mood
of 1922 when the Greek generals were blamed for the rout,
tried, and shot. Cavafy shares the violent outburst of popular
opinion which put the guilt on the generals, who may not have
been very competent, but hardly deserved so grim a fate, since
the real cause of defeat lay much deeper in the whole policy,
encouraged by Lloyd George, of trying to occupy Asia Minor.
But there is no doubt of the sufferings and the courage of the
Greek soldiers, ill-led and ill-supplied, against Kemal's ferocious
and fanatical army. Cavafy's tribute to the dead of the war is
in the spirit of an epitaph to the fallen such as might have been
written in almost any century of classical or Hellenistic Greece.
Its very bareness and spareness, its concentration on the single
theme of courage and the abiding memory of it, are derived from
the past and yet perfectly applicable to the present. Because
contemporary Greeks resemble their remote ancestors in a
time of disaster, Cavafy is able to write about them, but only
because he can identify the present with the past and give to it
a special independence which would be impossible for him if
he were to portray it just as it is. Cavafy is so determined to
make all experience true to his poetical self that he can treat
this public theme, which touches him deeply, only if he absorbs
it into his imaginative contact with the past. By setting the
disaster of 1922 in an age remote from his own he gives it a
special detachment and grandeur.

Cavafy's oblique approach to his subject is a variation on the
old device by which a contemporary event or issue is set in a

new and illuminating context by being related to a myth. This is common enough in classical Greek poetry, and Christian mythology is often used to illustrate some special point. The advantage of such a device is that some present theme gains in richness and reveals more clearly its universal character by being related to something outside the immediate moment. A striking example of it in recent times comes from far afield. Chinese poetry abounds in references both to history and to myth, and it is noteworthy that the Communist leader, Mao Tse-tung, who writes in the traditional style, sometimes uses them to illustrate a present occasion. In 1957 he wrote a short poem for his woman friend, Li Shu-yi, whose husband had fallen in battle against the Nationalists in 1933. Mao couples her with his own wife, who was killed by the war-lord Ho Chien in 1930, and celebrates both together:

> I lost my proud poplar, and you your willow;
> Poplar and willow soar to the heaven of heavens;
> Wu Kang, asked what he has to offer,
> Presents them with cassia wine.
>
> The lonely goddess in the moon spreads her ample sleeves
> To dance for these good souls in the endless sky;
> Of a sudden comes word of the Tiger's defeat on earth
> And they break into tears of torrential rain.[11]

Behind this lies an ancient myth. Wu Kang, who had sought immortality, was condemned by the gods to cut down the cassia-tree in the moon, but every time he fells it, it becomes whole again. Mao imagines that his own wife and his friend's husband are transported to the moon, where Wu Kang, freed at last from his toil, welcomes them. The goddess in the moon spreads her robes for a dance, and, on hearing of the defeat of the Tiger, of hostile forces on earth, all burst into tears of joy. The whole scheme fits together, and even the image of the Tiger is apt, since it too comes from legend and is easily given a new application. The special interest of Mao's myth is that he does not believe in it, but uses it to convey the undying glory which his own wife and his friend's husband have won. Mao, as we might expect, sometimes writes about public events in a perfectly straightforward manner and feels no qualms about it, but here he has chosen a myth because it exalts his subject and underlines elements which mean a lot to him. Its imagery is rich in associations, and the theme of dying for a cause is ennobled by them.

Poetical ideals and poetical traditions are not the only impediments between a poet and the treatment of public themes. The very complexity of the political scene may be such that he shrinks from speaking about it, and at times it may so intrude upon his inner self that in his distress at its horrors he becomes almost speechless. Though he must say something to ease his trouble, the hard business of composition is hampered by these disturbing forces, and he may even feel that he cannot fully tell the truth about them and must from sheer agony keep silence. This quandary lies behind the introductory poem of *Giorno dopo Giorno* (*Day after Day*), which Salvatore Quasimodo (b. 1901) wrote during the German occupation of Italy in the Second World War:

> E come potevamo noi cantare
> con il piede straniero sopra il cuore,
> fra i morti abbandonati nelle piazze
> sull'erba dura di ghiaccio, al lamento
> d'agnello dei fanciulli, all'urlo nero
> della madre che andava incontro al figlio
> crocifisso sul palo del telegrafo?
> Alle fronde dei salici, per voto,
> anche le nostre cetre erano appese,
> oscillavano lievi al triste vento.[12]

> *And how were we able to sing*
> *with the stranger's foot upon our hearts,*
> *among the dead abandoned in the squares*
> *on the grass hard with ice, to the lament*
> *like a lamb's of the children, to the black howl*
> *of the mother, who went to meet her son*
> *crucified on the telegraph-pole?*
> *On the branches of the willows, by our vow,*
> *our lyres also were hung,*
> *they swayed lightly in the black wind.*

When Quasimodo raises an age-old question and asks how he can sing in a strange land, it comes with all the greater poignancy because the land is his own, made strange by its sufferings and its horrors. He suggests that in a time like this even poetry is somehow a profanation of the dead, but he masters his misgivings and understands what the problem is. The lyres swaying lightly on the trees mean that poetry still comes to him, even though it comes without an impelling force, as a breath stirring in his sadness. He has found an answer to Eliot's negation, and it is that in such times the spirit of poetry, however discouraged, moves into action of its own accord and will not be denied.

A poet may defeat circumstances through his art, but if his art itself is threatened, his case is indeed hard. He knows that he must be free to maintain his inner life intact and to absorb and transform reality as his genius compels him. But if forces from without seek to interfere with him or to drive him into duties which he rejects as alien or false or unworthy, he is in an ugly quandary. He has to fight for his very existence as a poet, and perhaps no struggle demands so much from him or faces him with heavier decisions. He inevitably asks what his art is really worth and whether he should defend it at a heavy cost to his own peace and happiness. This was the predicament of Boris Pasternak (1890–1960).[13] Throughout his career he had tried not to compromise about his art, and when he had done so even on a very small scale, as in some poems of the Second World War, he felt that he had acted unworthily of his calling and that the results were inferior to what they ought to have been. But with a very few exceptions his poems were composed in strict obedience to what he thought poetry ought to be, and on this he shared to the full the high ideals of art which had prevailed in Russia before the Revolution. But in his last years, especially after 1946, he found himself restricted and discouraged on every side, dismissed by many of his contemporaries as a mere translator, and cut off from the popular acclaim which he deserved and could easily have won if his poems had been allowed to circulate. His artistic conscience forbade him to make any concessions or compromises, and his appalling predicament is revealed in the poems which he collected at the end of *Dr Zhivago* and which are quite as relevant to himself as to his imaginary hero, and in the series *When the Skies clear.*

Pasternak, driven back on his own resources, has come to see more clearly what his art really is and found that it is a religious activity. That is why he begins the poems of *Dr Zhivago* with a piece in which he compares himself with Hamlet, but at the same time with Christ, and this means that, though he is watched by a hostile audience, he feels himself to be a truthful witness to his time as only a dedicated poet can. This is his destiny, and he accepts it with patient resignation, knowing that he lives in an age of Pharisees and can do nothing but say so. His attitude is that of devout faith, but though he uses the imagery of Christianity, what fundamentally concerns him is the truth and the integrity of art, which he regards as a task divinely commanded. This is the creed which keeps him at work and consoles him for neglect and contempt. It may indeed mean that he is isolated and persecuted, but for this too he has a consolation. In 'My Soul'[14] he asserts his unity with countless friends who have been imprisoned or shot or driven to suicide, and though this still causes him deep distress and grief, he feels that their sufferings have not been useless, for their example will nourish the future and from them a new poetry will grow. At the same time his isolation has cost him dearly, not merely in his own happiness but in his contact with his fellow-men. In 'The Change' he looks back on his first ardent love of mankind and sees how it has been corrupted. He speaks of the time when he used to seek out the poor and the humble and tried to win their love, seeing in them an unaffected strength, but even this has been held against him, and his genuine compassion has been turned into an object of shame by men who enforce a mechanical optimism and find nothing good in suffering or in pity. In the result Pasternak finds himself cut off from his kind and robbed of the faith which he once had in them:

Всем тем, кому я доверял,
Я с давних пор уже невернен.
Я человека потерял,
С тех пор, как всеми он потерян.[15]

*In all in whom I put my trust*
*It has long vanished past recall;*
*And man has been completely lost*
*By me, since he was lost by all.*

In the general destruction of human values Pasternak too has lost his old affection for mankind. This has been forced on him by others, and he has nothing left but his art.

In these forbidding circumstances Pasternak concentrated on his art and believed that he had really found himself as an artist. He wrote with a new firmness and assurance and avoided some of the bolder devices which had enlivened his earlier poetry. Yet it is extremely hard for a man to work only for his own satisfaction, and Pasternak certainly would have profited from some recognition of his efforts. When he was offered the Nobel Prize for Literature in 1959, he felt at first that his long efforts had been recognised and compared his feelings with a bird singing in the woods, a road through trees in a thaw, a journey in a train through a world that is being remade.[16] His enforced solitude and self-sufficiency had after all not sufficed him and he rejoiced and expanded in regaining contact with the outside world and knowing that it appreciated his efforts. But the Nobel Committee had made an incredible blunder. In giving him the Prize they certainly mentioned his poetry but they also mentioned, with what looked like more emphasis, *Dr Zhivago*, and, since this, not very correctly, had been acclaimed everywhere as an anti-Soviet book, Pasternak was denounced in Russia for something very like treachery. The Union of Soviet Writers attacked him from all sides, and he was compelled to refuse the Prize. What seemed at first to be a blessing turned out to be a curse which hastened Pasternak's death and wrought havoc among those who were nearest and dearest to him.

Yet even now Pasternak clung to the hope that the storm had passed and that he would be able to pursue his work in peace, to cleanse everything from impurity and create a situation in which truth and magnanimity would prevail. But he soon saw how menacing his position was and in 'The Nobel Prize' he analyses his quandary. At the start he has no illusions about its gravity:

> Я пропал, как зверь в загоне.
> Где-то люди, воля, свет,
> А за мною шум погони,
> Мне наружу ходу нет.
>
> Темный лес и берег пруда,
> Ели сваленной бревно.
> Путь отрезан отовсюду.
> Будь что будет, все равно.[17]

> *Like a beast that's trapped, I've fallen.*
> *Somewhere are people, freedom, light;*
> *At my back the pack is calling,*
> *And for me there is no flight.*
>
> *Lakeside shore and darkest woodland,*
> *Gaunt trunk of a levelled tree;*
> *Every side escape is hopeless.*
> *Come what may, all's one to me.*

Then, for a moment, Pasternak asks whether he has not done something wrong and thinks that he must be a murderer or a criminal, since this would at least account for his treatment. But he knows that he is innocent and comforts himself with the knowledge that he has made the whole world weep over the beauty of his country. This is his consolation and his reward, and once he has reasserted himself with this confidence, he looks into the future. Though he himself is on the edge of the grave, he believes that in due time malice and evil will yield to the spirit of good, and he believes this because his art is a religion, which calls for divine help in its exercise and the divine virtues of truth and charity in all that he does. In the end Pasternak triumphs over his adversaries and his circumstances because his belief in art is a life-giving faith and embraces the whole of being. Though he has been threatened at its very centre, he has remained true to it, and from his last battle some of his finest poetry was born.

The more violent the impact of events is on a poet, and the more deeply he is committed to them, the more he needs some uniting idea or mood to master them and bring them to order. So the Greek poet George Seferis (b. 1900), faced by the tragic disasters of his country in the German invasion, wrote Ὑστερό-γραφο ('Postscript'), which is explained by the additional words 'September 11, 1941'. The poem was written immediately after the conquest of Greece by the Germans, and since Seferis was in Egypt at the time, we can construct its origin. His theme is starving children by whose appearance he is appalled and horrified, and his horror suggests what lies behind the heart-rending sight:

’Αλλὰ ἔχουν μάτια κάταspra χωρὶς ματόκλαδα
καὶ τὰ χέρια τους εἶναι λιγνὰ σὰν τὰ καλάμια.

Κύριε, ὄχι μ’ αὐτούς. Γνώρισα
τὴ φωνὴ τῶν παιδιῶν, τὴν αὐγὴ
πάνω σὲ πράσινες πλαγιὲς ροβολώντας
χαρούμενα σὰν μέλισσες καὶ σὰν
τὶς πεταλοῦδες, μὲ τόσα χρώματα.
Κύριε, ὄχι μ’ αὐτούς, ἡ φωνή τους
δὲ βγαίνει, κὰν ἀπὸ τὸ στόμα τους.
Στέκεται ἐκεῖ κολλημένη σε κίτρινα δόντια.[18]

*But they have eyes all white, without eyelashes*
*And their arms are thin as reeds.*

*Lord, not with these. I have known*
*The voice of children at dawn*
*Running on green hillsides*
*Happily coloured, like bees*
*And like the butterflies,*
*Lord, not with these, their voice*
*Cannot even leave their mouths.*
*It stays there glued on yellow teeth.*

Seferis cannot but compare the shrunken and shrivelled forms which he now sees with the children whom he remembers, and the contrast fills him with such dismay that he cannot endure

the sight and prays not to be forced to look at it. The birthright
of these spectres of humanity is to enjoy the sun and the wind,
and they have been robbed of it. In the spectacle of them
Seferis finds a terrible lesson, that, though men normally become by their own efforts what they wish to be, these are too
broken by their struggle to know it. In them he sees an example
of God's will being done, and he begs that it may be done in
some other way. His horror is not a conventional or even a usual
reaction, but rises from his agonised distress, and his extreme
honesty in saying just what he feels gives a powerful indi-
viduality to the poem. He too has a uniting principle, which is
more religious than metaphysical, but religious with a noble
independence. A sight all too common at the time is seen in
its terrible and tragic reality, and Seferis's interpretation of
it is a comment on what is happening in many parts of the
world.

In their different ways Pasternak and Seferis show how a
poet may be driven by agony of spirit to look at much wider
issues and to find a shaping thought for his treatment of them.
Yet even in the heyday of intimate poetry some poets were so
outraged by current events that they felt them as personal
issues, as well they might, for sooner or later they were to suffer
from them. In the thirties the menace of war and persecution
was far too real to be dismissed as an abstraction, and it is not
surprising that it became a matter for fear and indignation. To
grasp it in its entirety was almost impossible, but a poet could,
by applying his own convictions to this or that aspect, throw a
fierce light on its essential character. This was no time to echo
public opinion, and the poet had to rely on his own resources
and shape them into something which would be unique in its
unexpected contents. For very heterogeneous material he could
find a unity by relating it to something beyond his actual theme,
to an embracing notion, which might be metaphysical or religious or in some other way transcendent, and this would exalt
it beyond his personal limits and give a universal appeal to its
particular matter. This is what Dylan Thomas (1914–53) does

88

in a remarkable poem of the thirties, when the dictators had all at their feet and could settle anything by a mere assertion of their will:

> The hand that signed the paper felled a city;
> Five sovereign fingers taxed the breath,
> Doubled the globe of dead and halved a country;
> These five kings did a king to death.
>
> The mighty hand leads to a sloping shoulder,
> The finger joints are cramped with chalk;
> A goose's quill has put an end to murder
> That put an end to talk.
>
> The hand that signed the treaty bred a fever,
> And famine grew, and locusts came;
> Great is the hand that holds dominion over
> Man by a scribbled name.
>
> The five kings count the dead but do not soften
> The crusted wound nor stroke the brow;
> A hand rules pity as a hand rules heaven;
> Hands have no tears to flow.[19]

Behind this poem lie the treaties by which Hitler, using threats or cajolery, rearranged Europe to suit his own ambitions, but its details do not come from them or from immediate events. Hitler's treaties seldom put an end to murder, nor did his murders always put an end to talk, at least from him. Yet the poem is a correct and penetrating account of a state of affairs in which the will of a single man imposes itself on nations by the mere scrawling of a signature. This is the key to the poem, as it conveys a deadly, unrelenting mechanism at its hideous work.

Thomas succeeds not merely through his insight into the nature of absolute power and its consequences but because he relates it to something wider which gives it a special perspective and is very much his own contribution. When at the end he says

> A hand rules pity as a hand rules heaven,

he reaches his climax and calls for special attention. He means that the unrestrained ruler deals with pity as ruthlessly and impersonally as another unrestrained power deals with the universe. In neither case does pity count for anything, since all that matters is the exercise of power which demands unlimited surrenders and gets them by a mere gesture. This is not an ordinary point of view, and though Thomas may have got an inkling of it from Hardy, whom he much admired, it is still his own and all the more impressive because it is stated in this unobtrusive, unassuming way, as if everyone were in the secret. Thomas presents political power as a microcosm of a whole, indifferent, inexorable universe and thereby makes his immediate theme more forbidding and more frightening. He suggests that such power is ultimately invincible, that nothing can be done against it, that it lies outside human capacities and belongs to the very nature of things. The hand is the symbol of remote unfathomable forces, and though it belongs to a human being, it has in its ghastly, mechanistic behaviour ceased to be human. Thomas is concerned with brutal facts in a brutal universe, and it is this central conviction which gives shape to his poem, but its strength comes from his resistance to it, from his pity and compassion, his horror at the real nature of power as it has been revealed to his generation.

Yet not all situations can be brought under a single mood or idea, and some of considerable consequence and import yield no clear answer to the poet's probing. He sees them in their complexity and is fascinated by them, but hardly as a unity, certainly not as a unity with an ulterior significance. In these conditions he must make the most of what he sees and leave us to draw our conclusions. In such a task the modern technique is admirably helpful in catching fleeting moods and changing shades by an apt choice of imagery, and the more troubled a theme is, the greater is the challenge that it presents. The poet may find himself obsessed by a matter so complex that, though he does not see it as a whole, he finds in it much that troubles and provokes him. Few subjects could be more unmanageable than the German surrender at the end of the Second World War or invite more varied considerations. It was, for instance, possible for Hans Egon Holthusen (b. 1913) in 'Tabula Rasa'[20] to try to cover it in its whole range as a crisis in the history of man, and his attempt has the virtues of courage and candour. His sweeping generalities and his somewhat commonplace images are undeniably forceful, and though his manner is too reminiscent of Rilke's middle period, he does not overplay his part. Yet Holthusen seems old fashioned not merely in his manner but in his outlook. His effort to grasp in its main outlines a huge scheme of history is more than he can manage, and at no point does he surprise us by a sudden insight or touch us very deeply. In the end we feel that a poet of the nineteenth century would have done it better just because he dealt in large conceptions and customary emotions.

On the other hand so amorphous a subject presented many facets which were in themselves challenging and might in a skilful combination lead to illuminating results. So Hans Baermann Steiner (1909–52) wrote '8 Mai, 1945' about the German collapse, naming his poem from the day of the capitulation. This had few resemblances with the Armistice of 1918, and though it was the end of a shameful epoch, it was not easy to respond to it with any simplicity of mood. In many minds it provoked disparate and competing emotions, and it was almost impossible to think of its significance without remembering all that had preceded it for some twelve years. Steiner's poem is his response to an immediate situation, for which he may long have waited but which, when it comes, reveals unforeseen peculiarities. By his abrupt, fully charged sentences and his strongly contrasted images he conveys the paradoxes of the situation and hints at preceding history which is still in some sense at work:

Hastig ist der vogelflug. Weh, was jemals sich heben wollte,
Hat der steine gewicht,
Die unter der erde dauern, verkittert mit leibern und jahren der liebe.

Bürger begruben ihren ruchlos verzärtelten krieg.
Mohnblumen blühen aus bier.
Girlanden schnüren die leiber fiebernder haüser.

Die nassen fahnen tropfen in schwüle festluft.
Hinter dem trommelwirbel
Zickzackt ein eisläufer über gefrorenen blutsee.[21]

*The flight of birds is hurried. Alas, what ever wished to rise*
*Has the weight of stones*
*Which remain under the earth, cemented with bodies and years of love.*

*Civilians bury their wickedly pampered war.*
*Poppies blossom out of beer.*
*Garlands tie up the bodies of feverish houses.*

*The wet flags drip in the sultry festival-air.*
*Behind the roll of the drums*
*An ice-skater zigzags over a frozen lake of blood.*

Steiner finds little comfort and no exhilaration or even relief
in the end of the war, and knows very well that harsh prospects
lie ahead. His jerky, condensed, detached manner conveys the
mood of a man who is trying to master a very recalcitrant theme
and drives his way through it by a strong effort of intelligence,
observing salient points and fixing them in forcible, provocative
images. In the first verse the hurried flight of birds indicates
rapid change, but this is countered by a conviction, heavily
stressed, that any change worth having will indeed be difficult
because too much has been lost in a waste of life and of love.

In the second verse Steiner marks the contradictions between
the present and the immediate past. The civilians who have
given everything to the war now bury it and put it out of their
minds. If in the past they have been sodden with its intoxica-
tion, they now ask nothing for it but oblivion, and the feverish
houses decked with garlands are a symbol for the hysteria with
which people claim that all is well but fail to hide the fragility
of their pretences. Then the third verse gives, as it must, a
depressing, inconclusive end, which is the essence of the situation. The air of festivity is unhealthy and unreal. The old brutal
spirit is not dead but can still be heard in the roll of drums, and
efforts at recovery from the lurid past are as tentative and pre-
carious as a man skating over a lake of frozen blood. The poem
neither offers comfort nor strikes a tragic note; still less does it
exalt. It sees things as they are, in their confusion and squalor,
and presents the bleak, unredeemed aftermath of an age of
evil-doing. Steiner faces a very large and difficult issue, but by

his choice of a few illuminating points gives at least a revealing sketch of what the capitulation of Germany means.

If Steiner leaves us uneasy, we cannot complain, since that is plainly his intention. In some ways his mood recalls Eliot's in his uncomforting dissections of the modern soul, but it is more carefully focused and its imagery has a more immediate and more obvious reference. Because Steiner has mastered a painful situation for himself by looking courageously at it, he enables us to do the same and gives something worth having. Yet in him we miss that additional dimension which can give strength to political themes and set them in a wider scheme, thereby increasing their significance and their appeal. There are times when the modern technique of close and precise observation inhibits a more embracing view and discourages us from trying to see beyond the details to the whole, and we may feel that this is true of Steiner and others like him. They cannot be expected to write otherwise than they do, and their refusal to take a wider view is in a way a source of strength, since they thrive on restriction and limitation. They see so keenly what they see, and know it so well for what it is, because their whole attention is fixed on selected points. This means that their kind of poetry lacks onslaught and onrush. It brings its own rewards in sharpened insight and trained sensibility, but they are more often disturbing than exhilarating.

To illustrate how far some poetry has moved in this direction and how it dispenses with the powerful moods and the imaginative ideas which hold so much political poetry in control, we may take an example from the other end of the world to show how differently a passionate simplicity can achieve results. Though the Japanese domination of Korea was ruthlessly and brutally efficient, it could not kill Korean poetry, which in spite of it or because of it enjoyed a revival comparable to its finest days. Though more than twenty-five years were to pass before the 'Declaration of Independence', issued by writers and intellectuals in 1919, could be turned into reality, the poets never gave up hope and suffered heavily in imprisonment, torture, and death for their loyalty. How they envisaged it can be seen from a poem by Sim Hun (1904–37), who did not live to see his hope realised but imagined vividly what it would mean when it was:

When that day comes
Mount Samgak will rise and dance,
the waters of Han will rise up.

If that day comes before I perish,
I will soar like a crow at night
and pound the Chongno-bell with my head.
The bones of my skull
will scatter, but I shall die in joy.

When that day comes at last
I'll roll and leap and shout on the boulevard
and if joy still stifles within my breast
I'll take a knife

and skin my body and make
a magical drum and march with it
in the vanguard. O Procession!
Let me once hear that thundering shout,
my eyes can close then.[22]

Sim Hun is the antithesis of Steiner both in his mood and in his treatment of it. The prospect of some large but quite unspecified deliverance in the future calls for no such precision as suits a chaotic situation in the present. The Korean poet is not, like the German, tied to brutal facts, and all that matters for him is the excited, exalted mood which the thrilling prospect, however distant, awakes. He sets his vision in familiar surroundings with a Korean mountain and a Korean river and the Chongno-bell in the main square at Seoul. In claiming that nature will share his joy and rise and dance with him he uses a very ancient fancy which has parallels in the Psalms of David, and in an agreeable variation on 'the pathetic fallacy' embodies the notion that on high occasions the physical surroundings of men cannot fail to share their delight. But Sim Hun uses it for his own purpose. Since what he foresees is the liberation of Korea, the actual land will be freed with its inhabitants, and he shapes this into an image which all his countrymen, whatever their class or background, will understand. He finds the prospect so wildly exhilarating that he will lose himself in delight, and this he figures as a joy so violent that he will burst the confines of his body. He means something that we all know, that there are rapturous moments which are too much for us, and we feel that we are annihilated by them. Sim Hun picks up this idea and puts it into various shapes, all of which have a certain humorous exaggeration without abating any of their hints of incredible delight. He speaks very much for himself, but what inspires him is the perfectly simple prospect of a long-awaited deliverance from an implacable tyranny.

The contrast between Steiner and Sim Hun illustrates the advantages of a unifying idea. It pulls perceptions together and gives a shape to a poem. But it can do more than this. It can set a situation in such a perspective that it assumes a more clearly universal character and touches on something much more significant than the present moment. Poets, having re-fashioned their art on truth to their feelings and precision in the expression of them, have slowly and tentatively begun to treat public affairs with more sweep and more confidence. Some of the best living poets see their themes not merely as personal matters but as relevant to wider issues which set them in a large context. By this means they have resumed their old task of raising important problems for the heart or the conscience, as belonging to religion or morality or simple humanity. Thus in March 1939 George Seferis wrote Άνοιξη μ.Χ ('Spring A.D.') when the corruption and the cowardice of Europe lay heavily on his heart. He is wounded in his love of life and his compassion for the betrayed. The spring in which he writes becomes a symbol for the free and natural life which is denied by the actions of men, and especially by the older generation which is in control. The spring suggests joy and abundance and challenges the old men who, with their failing souls and minds and bodies, would be better dead. On this basis Seferis constructs the atmosphere of the time and shows how its hopes

95

are shattered by this withered spirit in high places. So far he might be taken to refer to no more than a general world-weariness, but then it emerges that he has something more immediate in his mind:

Μὲ τοὺς καινούργιους ροδαμοὺς
οἱ γέροντες ἀστόχησαν
κι' ὅλα τὰ παραδώσανε
ἀγγόνια καὶ δισέγγονα
καὶ τὰ χωράφια τὰ βαθιὰ
καὶ τὰ βουνὰ τὰ πράσινα
καὶ τὴν ἀγάπη καὶ τὸ βιὸς
τὴ σπλάχνιση καὶ τὴ σκεπὴ
καὶ ποταμοὺς καὶ θάλασσα·
καὶ φύγαν σὰν ἀγάλματα
κι' ἄφησαν πίσω τους σιγὴ
ποὺ δὲν τὴν ἔκοψε σπαθὶ
ποὺ δὲν τὴν πῆρε καλπασμὸς
μήτε ἡ φωνὴ τῶν ἄγουρων.[23]

*When the new shoots were bursting*
*The old men failed.*
*They surrendered everything*
*Grand-children, great-grand-children*
*The tilth of the pastures*
*The green of the mountains*
*Both love and livelihood*
*Both mercy and roof*
*Both rivers and sea;*
*They departed like statues*
*Leaving silence behind them*
*That was cut by no sword stroke*
*Broken by no galloping*
*Or voices of young men.*

This is how Seferis sees appeasement as it was practised by Great Britain and France in 1939. For him it is the betrayal of young life, a surrender of all that promises hope for the future, that offers warmth and affection and security. Yet, after he has denounced the old for their behaviour and spoken of the solitude and deprivation which follow in their wake, he sees that a new spirit is stirring among men and that the spring does not come in vain. It brings not comfort but effort and courage and turns the victims into martyrs. The executioner may get to work, but in the end he achieves nothing, for the common consciousness after the great betrayal cannot be broken by him. Seferis speaks from a personal agony, but it is also an agony of the western world, and though he is deeply troubled by it and not afraid to condemn those who are responsible for it, he subdues his doubts and fears, and forecasts what good will come out of evil. Few others would at this date have agreed completely with him, and yet this is no private whim but the deeply considered conclusion of a man who can get sufficiently away from his own involvement to think about the most vital issue of his time. What gives a special dimension to Seferis's poem is its trust, despite everything, in the human race, and this takes it beyond morality and beyond religion to a sphere where its theme is sanctified by the desire and the power to live.

This extension of personal feelings to a wide sphere is extremely hazardous unless the poet is so sure of his values that he can give assurance and clarity to outlooks which might otherwise be lost in a welter of emotions. The long tradition of Christianity provides a ready-made mythology which can still be used with powerful effect by setting a poet's thoughts against a familiar background. So one of the best poems directed against the Nazis is the work of a Roman Catholic, Werner Bergengruen (b. 1892). In the five stanzas of 'Die letzte Epiphanie' ('The last Epiphany') a nameless figure tells of his visits to 'dies Land', which is Germany. He loves it, and has not only sent it message after message but himself visited it in different shapes, but always with hideous consequences. In the first he came by night as a Jewish refugee, with tattered shoes, hunted, but they called for the police and thought that they were doing God a service. In the second he came as an old woman broken by anguish, but they talked about the future of the race, and gave back nothing but her ashes. In the third he came as a boy from the east, begging for bread, but they shrugged their shoulders and killed him. Then comes the last visit:

Ich kam als Gefangner, als Tagelöhner,
verschleppt und verkauft, von der Peitsche zerfetzt.
Ihr wandtet den Blick von dem struppigen Fröner.
Nun komm ich als Richter. Erkennt ihr mich jetzt?[24]

*I came as a captive, was hired day by day,*
*Was slashed by the whip, hawked for dealers to buy.*
*From the unkempt drudge your eyes turned away.*
*Now I come as a judge. Do you know—who am I?*

The figure who speaks in these successive shapes is Christ, who comes in four different incarnations as someone needy and persecuted, always to be treated with inhuman brutality, which may at first make excuses but in the end does not even try to do so. The different appearances stand not for any historical sequence of events but for Christ's attempts to test the Germans in their treatment of outcasts and refugees, whose sufferings he himself incarnates. The last epiphany, which gives the poem its title, comes with majesty and menace in the last line. Bergengruen moves inside a Christian scheme, and this makes it easier for him than if he had drawn on some system of his own invention. More than this, it allows him to identify his feelings with a scheme of values which anyone can understand and which carries many ancient and powerful associations. The personal touch is enriched and enlarged by this attachment to much wider issues, and the particular situation assumes a universal importance. Bergengruen's achievement is not ordinarily at this high level, but here he has been inspired by his horror of Nazi atrocities to speak with a masterful authority and conviction.

The advantage of a traditional imagery is that it engages even those who do not accept its full presuppositions but preserve enough relics of sympathy to respond to its emotional appeals. It cannot of course be of a very specialised or restricted kind, and it need not have any precise theological content. Indeed it may be even more effective when it is only an ingredient in some complex construction, in which other ingredients come from other sources and increase the poet's appeal by their reference to various traditions assimilated in the mixed culture of the west. So in the Second World War, seeing with his own eyes the sorrows and sufferings of Italy, Quasimodo looks beyond them to the vast brutality of his time and laments that man has never really changed his nature. Quasimodo conveys deep feelings, an innate sense of right and wrong, a compassion for the pitiful state of man, and a horror for the excesses of which he is capable. In him various currents of thought unite, and so naturally are they combined and so true are they to the human heart that we feel no discord or inconsistency between them. In 'Uomo del mio tempo' ('Man of my time') he concentrates his feelings in a short space with a remarkable tension and power:

Sei ancora quello della pietra e della fionda;
uomo del mio tempo. Eri nella carlinga,
con le ali maligne, le meridiane di morte,
— t'ho visto — dentro il carro di fuoco, alle forche,
alle ruote di tortura. T'ho visto; eri tu,
con la tua scienza esatta persuasa allo sterminio,
senza amore, senza Cristo. Hai ucciso ancora,
come sempre, come uccisero i padri, come uccisero
gli animali che ti videro per la prima volta.
E questo sangue odora come nel giorno
quando il fratello disse all'altro fratello:
'Andiamo ai campi'. E quell'eco fredda, tenace,
è giunta fine a te, dentro la tua giornata.
Dimenticate, o figli, le nuvole di sangue
salite dalla terra, dimenticate i padri:
le loro tombe affondano nella cenere,
gli uccelli neri, il vento, coprono il loro cuore.[25]

*You are still he of the stone and the sling,*
*man of my time. You were in the cock-pit,*
*with the malignant wings, with the meridians of death,*
*—I have seen you,—inside the waggon of flame, at the gallows,*
*at the wheels of torture. I have seen you; it was you,*
*with your exact science persuaded to destruction,*
*without love, without Christ. You have killed again,*
*as always, as your fathers killed, as they killed*
*the animals who saw you for the first time.*

*And the smell of this blood is as on the day*
*when the brother said to the other brother:*
*'Let us go to the fields.' And that echo, cold, clinging,*
*has come at last to you, within your day.*
*Forget, o sons, the clouds of blood*
*risen from the earth, forget your fathers:*
*their tombs sink in the ashes,*
*the black birds, the wind, cover their hearts.*

The central, informing idea, that man has always thirsted for blood, is Quasimodo's own, and it is stated boldly at the start, as the inspiring and uniting theme of the poem. We are shocked into attention by the statement that man is still what he was in the Stone Age, at the beginning of history, and the perennial nature of the theme is enforced by images drawn from the destruction of animals and the murder of Abel by Cain, which are the ancient equivalents of the modern dropping of bombs by aeroplanes. The habit of bloodshed is like an echo haunting the ear or like clouds of blood risen from the earth, and the call to forsake the old murderous ways reaches its finale in an impassioned appeal against all such slaughter and a hope that, like our forefathers who taught and practised it, it will sink into oblivion. In his imagery Quasimodo stresses the essential simplicity and the wide human relevance of his theme. Everyone can understand him, and his feelings are ultimately those of any compassionate man. The horror of the unending slaughter, which changes its shape but does not change its character, enables him to give his whole poetical self to a theme which has no limits in place or in time and is more than ever hideous in our own age.

Seferis and Quasimodo have both recovered some of the spaciousness of the nineteenth century without falling into its artificial abstractions, but they have at the same time kept the richness of texture and the variety of movement which are the special virtues of the modern personal manner. They say nothing which they have not thought out with their own full natures or presented with the most careful precision in shades of feeling and sensibility. They provide a practical answer to

Eliot's conviction that 'War is not a life: it is a situation'. For them war, as they foresee or experience it, has become part of their lives, and they have so mastered its disturbing menaces that it contributes to their inner being and even enriches it. In turning it into poetry they have done what their generation needed, and in retrospect Eliot's denial looks a little inhuman. Yet the effort has been very great, and it can never be easy to advance from the fine examination of the self to the large issues which public events raise. Nor does this kind of response come readily to modern poets who have been trained in a more sheltered and more domestic school. The remarkable thing is that it has happened, and for this we must be deeply grateful. But there remain other poets who do not fit into this scheme and have tried to evolve quite different methods of dealing with the world in which they live and with whose affairs they are actively concerned.

CHAPTER 4

# CONFLICTS AND UNCERTAINTIES

The highly personal poetry which we have considered has evoked violent opposition in more than one quarter. It has been variously denounced as hermetic, decadent, unintelligible, formalistic, and bourgeois. Not all attacks come from the same quarter, but while advocates of tradition complain of its lack of art, advanced critics complain that it has too much. And of course it is open to serious charges. Just because it is so personal, it does not rise readily to the challenge of public occasions, and only its most inspired exponents are able to do so. It is intended for a public so well educated that it can without much trouble grasp the most diaphanous allusions and sympathise with esoteric or exotic frames of mind. For this reason its public has seldom been as large as that of the more notable performers in the nineteenth century, and most of us must at times have felt that such poetry is in danger of inbreeding and becoming more and more the preserve of a few, initiated experts. This has outraged and exacerbated the politically minded who think that poets should speak for a whole contemporary situation, and especially those who, being themselves revolutionaries, wish to enlist poets on their side. Nor is this unreasonable. A revolution may provide some enthralling subjects for poetry, and we should expect powerful responses to it. The early years of the Russian Revolution certainly released many unsuspected talents and provoked from all angles an abundant and exhilarating poetry. But the demand for such poetry has been shaped in a very limited form, and this has led to much failure and error. Since revolutions claim to be made on behalf of the proletariat, it is assumed that in the new society at which they aim the arts must be in some sense proletarian. Though at the start their existing forms are highly unpromising, it is hoped that a truly popular art will somehow emerge. The notion is in itself nebulous, and the results have too often been confusion, disappointment, resentment, persecution, disaster, and death.

In Western Europe proletarian poetry is extremely rare and comes into existence only in very special circumstances. An outstanding example are some songs current in the British Army in the First World War. These are the authentic composition of fighting soldiers, and they owe nothing to cultivated poetry of the traditional kind or even to the songs of music-halls. They are latter-day folk-songs, born in very unusual conditions to meet urgent and immediate needs. The names of their authors are not known, and their actual texts have been subjected to the alterations and additions which are inseparable from any oral tradition, whether it be in heroic epic or in Victorian limericks. Yet despite their lack of formal distinction and conscious art, they have a surprising richness of content. Their strength is that they reveal a consciousness in which unresolved contradictions are entirely appropriate to men caught in circumstances which they cannot escape or control. Though their form and their language are extremely simple, the states of mind which they record are not. Some of them are remarkable for their deep feelings and for a sharp candour in dealing with them. Their peculiar quality is their fusion of self-mockery with self-pity. Self-pity is not in itself an attractive trait, but when anyone who suffers from it laughs at himself, it is transformed, and the result can be not only touching but powerful. It is the response of men to an intolerable situation which they see in all its odiousness but by which they refuse to be completely defeated. Through song they form an attitude which keeps them sane. Such songs vary in their devices, and the mixture is not always the same. 'Send out the Army and the Navy' begins with a mocking parody of a patriotic song, and then ends beautifully and brilliantly with the truth—'But for Gawd's sake don't send me'. 'Oh my, I don't want to die', first heard at Victoria Station in the winter of 1915 after the appalling slaughter at Loos, is on the surface a pure cry of complaint, but is also mocking and half-humorous. The more famous 'Oh, oh,

oh, it's a lovely war' handles with devastating irony the unlimited tedium of army life. These songs are without question
proletarian, and they are rich in a section of human experience
which we find in almost no other literature.

These songs belong to history. They throw light on what
soldiers actually felt, and they help to explain why men were
able to endure the war as long as they did. But they are an
isolated phenomenon which died with its unique circumstances
and had no influence on the more self-conscious poetry of war.
Something of the same kind happened in the American depres-
sion of 1929 and afterwards, and though the note then was not
so much irony and mockery as bleak misery, some of the songs
have a like intensely poignant note. But they too have made no
impression on poetry in general and are remembered, if at all,
for their human and historical interest. The same seems to be
true of other western countries, and after all it is to be expected.
The existence of a large and self-conscious middle-class has
restricted proletarian song to narrow limits, which tend, with
the extension of education on a national model, to become even
narrower. Our main poetical tradition owes little to popular
origins and has been shaped and disciplined by standards
derived from the aristocratic ideals of the Renaissance, and
even the most revolutionary poets have preferred to write in
this manner, reckoning perhaps that it will appeal to a wider
public and win greater attention.

Yet the conditions which prevail in Western Europe need
not prevail everywhere. There are some countries where social
classes are so separated that there is very little overlap between
a highly educated minority, which regards poetry much as we
do, and a proletariat, which has its own folk-songs and is quite
ready to express political aspirations and defeats in them. Such
not long ago was the position in Cuba. The traditional *son*
provides a form in which almost anything can be said, and since
it is meant to be sung, it sets a pattern for word-rhythm which
has to be followed. Nicolas Guillén (b. 1904) has consciously
assumed the role of a proletarian poet and made admirable use

of the means at his disposal. Of mixed Spanish and African descent, he has created his own poetry from the *son*. Though this is tempered by remote and not very visible influences from Europe and salted with a small pinch of Marxism, which does not, however, spoil the taste, it is popular, proletarian, and yet highly personal. Guillén's light, sprightly, dancing metres echo Cuban song, his language is that of lively talk, and even his brilliant and provocative imagery is drawn not from literature but from common speech. Because he sees political problems from the inside as single, concrete issues, of which he and his fellows are the victims, he adds to each his own touch of pathos or irony or mockery. He catches a whole integrated mood and presents complex situations with a compelling directness, as when in 'Soldado muerto' ('Dead Soldier') he conveys the appalling indifference with which a soldier's death is greeted. His girl and his mother do not matter; his captain gives brisk orders for his funeral, and the poem ends on the cruel line:

> Que más soldados tenemos.[1]
>
> *We've got plenty of soldiers.*

When he spreads himself on a wider scale in 'Visita a un Solar' ('Visit to a Tenement'), Guillén presents the actuality of a tenement by his brief, brilliant, and disturbing sketches of those who live in it and what their sufferings are.[2] His unusual mixture of revolt and melancholy hits off the spirit of a submerged class. He speaks for many beside himself, but his utterance remains very much his own. So in 'Cantaliso en un Bar' ('Song in a Bar') he contrasts his own existence with that of Americans, whose lot is very different from his:

> Todos estos yanquis rojos
> son hijos de un camarón,
> y los parió una botella,
> una botella de ron.
> ¿Quién los llamó?
> ¡Ustedes viven,
> me muero yo,

comen y beben,
pero yo no,
pero yo no,
pero yo no![3]

*All those red Yankees*
*are sons of a shrimp,*
*and a bottle gave them birth,*
*a bottle of rum.*
*Who told them to come?*
*You live,*
*and I die,*
*you eat and drink,*
*but not I,*
*but not I,*
*but not I!*

Guillén's art is not a reversion to popular methods, nor even a survival of them; it is an authentic extension of them to meet needs which have long been met in this way but not with this degree of attention and skill. Guillén sees that the traditional Cuban *son* is the right instrument for himself because he has it in his bones and his blood moves to its rhythms. He makes it work hard and gets many new effects from it, but they are such as his countrymen will understand at once, and through this complete unity of outlook Guillén succeeds in being a truly proletarian poet who does not allow social theories to interfere with his poetical methods.

In Cuba this is no doubt possible because the proletariat is in a large majority and cherishes its traditional songs. We might therefore expect something of this kind to have happened in Russia with the Revolution. There existed a truly proletarian literature both in the villages and in the cities. It included folk-epics, factory-songs, dance-songs, rhymed fables, and a variety of political verse varying from ephemeral squibs to weighty propaganda. The factory-songs were lively enough for Blok to use some of their measures and manner in *The Twelve*, while Demyan Bedny (1883–1945) for many years did useful, if not distinguished, work by writing old-fashioned fables on topical issues. Into some of his pieces he puts a nice touch of satire, as when he mocks a landowner for having planted fir-trees which in time grow into clubs with which he himself is beaten, or compares the 'Nepman' of Lenin's New Economic Policy with sheep whose wool is allowed to grow that in due course it may be sheared for the benefit of others. But this was not the kind of poetry that the authorities encouraged, and Bedny was, rightly enough, not regarded as a poet of the first importance. The history of poetry in Russia after the Revolution is various and dramatic and depressing, but not in the least what might have been foretold.

In its first years the Revolution had the best poets on its side. Men, like Mayakovsky, who had suffered from censorship and imprisonment, were passionately in favour of it and assumed that they could now say what they liked. So for a short time they could, and from 1917 to 1925 poetry had a lively and adventurous career. Trotsky, who overvalued some of his discoveries, thought that a political revolution meant a revolution in literature and gave his full support to Symbolists, Acmeists, Futurists, and Imagists, and any other poets who had something original to say. While Andrei Bely saw in the Revolution the coming of a Kingdom of Heaven on earth, Bryusov, who guessed quickly enough in which direction the wind was blowing, did his best to write on contemporary themes. But disasters soon came thick and fast. Blok lost his first faith in the Revolution, fell into a tragic silence, and died broken-hearted in 1921. In the same year Nikolai Gumilev was shot for taking part in a counter-revolutionary plot, and though the facts are still obscure, it is just what he might have done. The peasant-poet, Sergei Esenin (1895–1925), who had a wonderfully musical and spontaneous gift for lyrical song, believed in an ideal Russia ruled by peasants, but the subject did not awake his best talents, and he himself frustrated them even more. He found consolation in drink and the company of the dancer Isadora Duncan, though neither understood the other's language. A visit to the United States with her in the time of Prohibition undermined his health, and the crisis came when he appeared in the hall of the Hôtel Crillon in Paris wearing nothing but a top-hat. He returned, much damaged, to Russia, and though for a time his genius revived, he found the scene desperately depressing, and soon after Christmas 1925 hanged himself from the hot water-pipes in the Hôtel Angleterre in Leningrad with the rope of his trunk. As there was no ink available, he wrote before his death a deeply touching poem in his own blood, and the second stanza says:

> До свиданья, друг мой, без руки и слова,
> Не грусти и не печаль бровей, —
> В этой жизни умирать не ново,
> Но и жить, конечно, не новей.[4]

> *Now good-bye, my friend, no hand clasped, no word spoken,*
> *Do not let me vex or sadden you.*
> *In this life there's nothing new in dying,*
> *And, in truth, to live is not more new.*

It is true that Esenin's melancholy was aggravated by drink, but the Revolution had ceased to mean anything to him, and he had lost all desire for life.[5] Within a few years of the Revolution the scene had been transformed, and for a moment it looked as if a new generation must take up the tasks left by the old. Some good poets had gone into exile, with the inevitable loss of touch which comes with it, but in Russia events called as much as ever for a vigorous treatment. Yet the story of Russian poetry after 1925 is dismal beyond words. There was no lack of talent, even of genius, but in different ways it was silenced, forced or bribed to write on unsuitable subjects, and reduced to discipline by methods which killed originality. The Revolution came when Russia had a remarkable array of good poets, and one of its most successful policies was to stifle them and to put in their place a team of ventriloquist's dummies.

Though directed from above, this disastrous process was accelerated by the poets themselves, who, having expected some miraculous renewal of life, were soon disillusioned by bitter facts and felt that they were not wanted. Khlebnikov, who had been soldiering in Persia, returned home to find that nobody was interested in him or in his remarkable experimental

art. Even his fierce, rhapsodic poems on the Revolution made
no impression, and though, when he died, a young man, in
1922, the main reason was broken health and starvation, this was
made worse by a conviction that his worth was not recognised
and that his country felt no need for him. In what was almost
his last poem he passes a verdict on his life's work and leaves
no doubt about his failure to win recognition or the reason
for it:

Еще раз, еще раз,
Я для вас
Звезда.
Горе моряку, взявшему
Неверный угол своей ладьи
И звезды:
Он разобьется о камни,
О подводные мели.
Горе и вам, взявшим неверный угол сердца ко мне:
Вы разобьетесь о камни
И камни будут надсмехаться
Над вами,
Как вы надсмехались
Надо мной.[6]

*Once again, once again,*
*For you I'm*
*A star.*
*Woe to the sailor who has taken*
*The wrong angle of his ship*
*On a star:*
*He will be shattered on rocks,*
*On sand-banks below water.*
*Woe to you who have taken the heart's wrong angle on me.*
*You will be shattered on rocks,*
*And the rocks will laugh*
*Over you*
*As you used to laugh*
*Over me.*

Khlebnikov, with perfect justice, sees that he has been mis-
judged by his countrymen and that his work has been in vain.
Yet he is also right in foreseeing that in due course he will be
recognised, and this is just what happened. Once he was dead,

he could safely be praised as a leading poet of the Revolution, but in the meanwhile it was prudent to leave him alone. He compared himself with a star because he had foretold what wonders the future would bring, but this was too fanciful for his realistic masters, and he knew it.

More controversial and more tragic is the career of Mayakovsky. As a young man he had an extraordinary lyrical gift which added greatly to the richness of his first poetry. When the Revolution came, he wrote, as we have seen, about its splendid prospects. For a short time he was able to combine his very unusual genius with the demands of the time and to enrich the Revolution with his inimitable ebullience and fancy. But he felt that this was not enough and that he must turn his gifts to immediate and more mundane purposes. He wrote rhymed slogans, advertisements, and a long series of poems on transitory topical subjects, in which he defended the Soviets against critics at home or abroad, or urged his countrymen to adopt this or that line of conduct. He lectures his fellow-writers on their public duty, derides the dead Esenin for running away from life, even doubts whether Russia really needs poets. These pieces were written for public recitation, at which Mayakovsky was a consummate performer. His huge build, his formidable appearance, his resonant voice and his splendid command of rhythm made them very effective propaganda. Nor are they bad. They have many moments of ingenuity, eloquence, humour, and fancy. His long poem written after the death of Lenin maintains a noble austerity and self-control. But these poems are not the full, authentic voice of Mayakovsky, since from them he excludes much that is most original in his gifts. That he had not lost these gifts was clear when in 1928 he wrote his 'Letter to Comrade Kostrov on the Nature of Love',[7] which revives his old pathos and irony and candour. Mayakovsky seems to have persuaded himself that a true Soviet poet should not be tormented by love into writing about it, but on this occasion he yielded to something stronger than himself, not without justifiable misgivings. He did not sell out to the Soviets;

he gave his services freely because he thought that they would help his country. Since he addressed the proletariat in its own interest and almost in its own voice, he created a truly popular poetry, which despite its originality made an enormous impact. Up to a point he felt that he was doing the right thing, perhaps the only possible thing, but for himself it ended in tragedy.

On 14 April 1930 Mayakovsky shot himself. His action was unconditionally condemned by orthodox Marxists and was indeed sadly inconsequential in a man who had five years earlier derided Esenin for doing very much the same thing. But after his death the government could not restrict the sale of his books, and he was enthroned in the pantheon of Russian writers when Stalin unexpectedly announced that he 'was and remains the best and most talented poet of our Soviet epoch' and that 'indifference to his memory and his work is a crime'.[8] This was the beginning of the process of which Pasternak wrote: 'he began to be introduced forcibly, like potatoes under Catherine the Great. This was his second death; he had no hand in it.'[9] But Mayakovsky's suicide, which was so ably misrepresented by public announcements, is more interesting than this. Though we never really know why anyone kills himself, Mayakovsky had reasons for doing so. It does not matter that at the time he was unhappily in love. He had often been in love, and nearly always unhappily, but he had not shot himself for it. What is clear is that he had long suffered from an inner struggle between his desire to write the real poetry of which he knew himself to be capable and the compulsion, both from within and without, to write public pieces for the national benefit. In 1930 he was under harsh criticism even for writing as he did, and he might well complain that all his efforts to do the right thing had been futile and were now condemned. He had prostituted his art to no purpose, and not even been thanked for it. This is clear from 'Во весь голос' ('At the Top of my Voice'), which he wrote in the January before his death and in which he says quite unequivocally:

Но я
     себя
         смирал,
              становясь
на горло
         собственной песне.[10]

*But I*
    *subdued*
        *myself,*
            *and set my heel*
  *on the throat*
      *of my very own song.*

Mayakovsky has the air of taking this quite lightly or at least of thinking that it was worth the price, and that he does not deeply regret it. This was far from true. The struggle which this sacrifice set up in his inner consciousness was the cause of his death. He had given way as far as he possibly could, and now he could not face the prospect of submitting to the even stricter discipline which was demanded of him, and betraying the last vestiges of his artistic conscience. This is clear from the various drafts of an unfinished poem which was written just before his death. It seems to have been started as an epilogue to 'At the Top of My Voice', but it turns into an entirely personal message:

Как говорят, инцидент исперчен.
Любовная лодка разбилась о быт.[11]

*As they say, the incident is closed.*
*Love's boat has smashed on the daily round.*

This has been taken to mean that Mayakovsky's most recent love affair has failed because of moral disapproval of it. But there is no reason to think that this was so, or that he thought that it was. What he means is that with the new restrictions placed on him he cannot write about love as he knows that he must and that for this reason his whole creative being is ruined. The conflict between his devotion to his art and his public responsibilities is too much for him. The closed incident is his life.

Mayakovsky at least did his best to do what the authorities wanted, and though it killed him he had a kind of posthumous rehabilitation, which admitted that he had not sacrificed himself in vain. But his death, which is the end of a chapter, is also the start of a new chapter more dismal and more depressing. Poets cannot be stopped from writing poetry, but they can be stopped from having it published, and from 1930 onwards the Soviet government pursued a policy which insisted that only such poetry should be published as won official approval. The knowledge that his work may never see the light of day is a grave deterrent to even the most single-minded writer, and official psychology knew this and took advantage of it. Such men were to be extinguished by neglect, while those who were ready to do what was asked from them were to be looked after and rewarded. The policy towards literature was conscious and deliberate and had two sides. First, it was assumed that writers must not attack the régime, and this is understandable both in the early years of Communism, when the government was really in danger, and later, when persecution-mania had become so integral to the official mentality that conspiracies were suspected on every side. In the last resort control was left to the security police who found invaluable agents in the Union of Soviet Writers, many of whom soon saw that their comfort and survival depended on complete subservience and were quite happy to denounce one another for political heresy. When a system assumes that he who is not with it is against it, there is little hope of independence. So far policy, though conducted in defiance of the first revolutionaries, was in its appalling way consistent. This was the negative side of the matter, but there was also a positive side, a line of attack which sought to make literature an instrument of public policy. This too had happened before in revolutionary situations and was to be expected in Russia, but the shape it took was unforeseen and still provokes amazement. The general theory was that since Russia was a socialist state, it must have a literature which dealt truthfully with contemporary issues, and this was defined as Socialist

Realism. This sounds fair enough, but the application of the theory to practice bore no relation to its high-sounding claims. By Realism the authorities meant neither the new techniques of recent movements nor anything related to proletarian writing. They meant the conventional art of the later nineteenth century, no more and no less. Its forms had been outmoded long before the Revolution and gave no incentive to anything creative. They were bad enough for the novel, but worse for poetry, which needs constantly to renew itself by experiment and change if it is to keep its authentic life. Of course the Soviet authorities might have claimed that this was the kind of thing that the average Russian liked and that for this reason he must be provided with it. But even this may be doubted. It is not at all clear that the Russian public liked it. They accepted it because it was the only poetry available, but when some rare chance offered something better, they grasped it eagerly. When Pasternak recited his poems in public in Moscow, the audience called for 'encores' and refused to listen to inferior writers who wrote in the approved style. In these conditions, though an enormous amount of verse was published, very little of it was at all good, simply because the manner demanded was not one in which a modern man can express himself sincerely. Even if a poet's views were impeccably orthodox, and this was not easy because orthodoxy was always changing its demands, his style must have no hint of modernity. In the result Russians were compelled to write in a style reminiscent of Felicia Hemans, whose boy on the burning-deck would have been a suitable hero for Soviet youth-clubs. Though Marxism demands that art should have a social result, this art had almost no result at all. It was to some very small degree an anodyne, an up-to-date application of Anatole France's verdict that 'reading is the opium of the west', but it was no more than that. It neither explained nor inspired, and it did nothing to make Soviet society intelligible either to itself or to the outside world.

The vicious consequences of this policy were what we might expect. It silenced anyone who might be thought independent or lukewarm towards the régime. Anna Akhmatova was stopped from publishing in the middle twenties, and except for a brief spell in the Second World War, was condemned to silence until in 1964, on her seventy-fifth birthday, she was 'rehabilitated', with what advantages is not yet clear. She was not an enemy of the government, and her criticisms are not so much criticisms as personal regrets. If she was never much in favour of the new order, she was never militantly against it, but accepted it fatalistically as an ordeal to be endured. With Stalin's reign of terror the situation grew worse. Osip Mandel'shtam was kicked to insanity and death by the political police, and Marina Tsvetaeva (1892–1941), who was much admired by Pasternak and had returned from exile in 1939, killed herself two years later. The war brought some alleviation and even saw the emergence of some new, if not very distinguished, talent, but this was only a temporary abatement, and in August 1946 Andrei Zhdanov attacked two Leningrad journals and, with Stalin's full support, laid down the policy for literature:

The task of Soviet literature is to help the state to educate youth correctly, to answer its requirements, to bring up the new generation to be strong, believing in its cause, not fearing obstacles, ready to overcome all obstacles.

(*Pravda*, 21 August 1946)

Incidentally he delivered a personal onslaught on Akhmatova, whom he called 'part nun and part harlot, or rather both harlot and nun, in whom harlotry is mingled with prayer', and we must remember that to him harlots and nuns were equally objectionable. Not only has no such view of literature been produced since Plato, who after all was in no position to put it into effect and at least knew what literature was, but Zhdanov did not understand the elements of the matter if he thought that any poetry worthy of the name can be written to order for political ends. From 1946 to 1953 Russian poetry passed through its blackest and bleakest years, and very little printed was worth reading.

Since 1953, when Stalin died, the situation has slightly, but only slightly, improved. Soviet officials have at least realised that, even if literature is to perform the dreary tasks demanded of it, it must have some kind of distinction to recommend it to a people naturally addicted to the arts and capable of discrimination in them. More important, the younger generation has begun to assert itself, sometimes to its own harm. Alexander Esenin-Volpin (b. 1925), a natural son of Sergei Esenin, has written with great courage and frankness about matters which he knows to be abhorrent to his masters, and though his poems have not been published in Russia, they have had a wide circulation in private. He is a true individualist, who cannot refrain from saying what he thinks, and since this is often of a kind that is not officially admitted to exist, he has almost from the start been a victim of persecution. War and prison strengthened him in his opposition, and his refusal to conform may be seen in one of his latest poems, which begins:

О сограждане, коровы и быки!
До чего вас довели болшевики...

...Но еще начнется страшная война,
И другие постучатся времена...[12]

*My countrymen, oxen and cows, can you*
*See what the Bolsheviks have brought you to?*

*But there will come again a hideous war,*
*And other times will then knock at the door.*

Esenin-Volpin announces that in this new war he will have no thought for Russia, and his one wish is that his ashes shall not rest in Russian soil. It is not surprising that he has been eliminated from the literary scene. Since in theory the Soviet Union no longer has political prisoners, he is confined to a mental home from which he is occasionally released under strict supervision to help with calculations needed to send missiles into space. In an Introduction to his poems he says: 'There is no freedom of the press in Russia, but who can say that there is no freedom of thought?'[13] He at least seems able to show that this is true, but news from him comes very rarely, and nothing is known of his more recent poetry, if indeed he has written any.

A more cheerful record is that of two poets who were both born in 1933 and have both grown up since the end of the Second World War. Evgeny Evtushenko and Andrei Voznesensky are true poets, very differently gifted, but both serious artists and in their limits determined to speak the truth. Evtushensko recently said to a French journalist: 'I never write to order and work to no plan of production',[14] and in one poem he speaks of himself as listening to the noise of trams and trees and men that he may become like them and speak for them; Voznesensky knew Pasternak in his last years, learned much from him, and is not afraid to say so. Evtushenko has a resonant forceful language, and an ability to hammer a point home; Voznesensky has many tricks of alliteration and play with words and is by no means easy at a first reading. Both have been criticised for Formalism, and both have dismissed the charge with contempt, as if it were a matter of no importance. Both write about politics and show a certain independence in doing so. In denouncing Stalinism Evtushenko has been accused of building up his own personality, and in denouncing anti-Semitism, of anti-Leninist provocation—a dishonest but none the less dangerous charge. Voznesensky is the better poet of the two and capable of truly original and striking effects. But both poets are very much the product of their circumstances. Evtushenko claims with some reason to speak for the younger generation in Russia. He is deeply patriotic but insists that the Russian people is really international at heart. He writes on topics like Cuba and Algeria, and though what he says has an independent air, it none the less conforms to what most of his countrymen have been brought up to believe. He insists that poetry must be serious and that he will not squander his vocation on trifles, and he demands that old and young should say of him 'This is indeed a communist poet'.[15] Voznesensky also writes about politics and is as deeply imbued with Soviet ideas as Evtushenko. He made a name for himself with a long poem on Lenin, which, despite considerable eloquence and ingenuity, is profoundly conformist at heart. His dislike and distrust of the West are obvious, and there is no reason to think that he indulges them just to gain popularity. Recently he wrote a poem on the death of Marilyn Monroe, in which he saw yet another symptom of the decay of the West. This was not absurd or dishonest, for the suicide clearly indicated something very wrong somewhere. But Voznesensky overplays his hand when he sees a portent of 'a universal Hiroshima' and makes the dying actress forecast 'suicides, suicides everywhere'. Both poets show what Russia lost in the long years in which Stalin repressed the creative spirit. They pick up Russian poetry where it stopped in the twenties and start again from that point. Both are deeply committed in principle to Communism, which educated them and made them what they are, but they have the courage of their convictions, and despite many hindrances and annoyances they are not lickspittles or time-servers but speak for themselves at a level of accomplishment which, apart from Pasternak, has not been seen in Russian poetry for over thirty years. But magnificent chances have been lost, and Russian poets who now write about politics have nothing of the superb confidence and independence with which Blok faced the destiny of his country.

The failure of the Russians to create any true poetry in the Stalinist epoch and its surviving repercussions illustrate a point which is not to their liking. Even if we include Evtushenko and Voznesensky, it is clear that Russian poets are in no real sense proletarian. Whatever their own origin may be, their work owes very little indeed to the folk-songs and factory-songs of the Russian people. Nor would the Russian people wish for this. The enormous popularity of books by the new poets shows how greatly Russians care for poetry, but it is for poetry which has grown from a rich literary tradition, owes much to Mayakovsky and Pasternak, and is judged on its aesthetic merits. If it has a political content, that is all the better, but this must be presented in a truly poetical spirit. The new poetry is not bourgeois in any political sense; even in a strictly literary sense it is bourgeois only in so far as its roots are in Russian poetry of the nineteenth century, which was in fact more often written by aristocrats than by bourgeois. The word has been worked to death, and the only point of reviving it is to show that in their years of repression the Russians encouraged a poetry which was indeed bourgeois in the most pejorative sense—unadventurous, conventional, sentimental, and uninspired. What the Russian example really teaches is that good poetry will always win against bad, and that no orders from on high can make poetry good. The public assimilates without any obvious effort new and even difficult manners of writing, and is much happier with something that really excites it than with a repetition of worn-out themes in a worn-out style.

If a country like Russia, where the Revolution was successful, made these appalling mistakes, it was not likely that other countries, where old systems of government still prevailed, would be likely to produce poets who could present revolutionary themes without some sacrifice of their art. Russia was too patently their model for them to go their own way, and Russian theories about the usefulness of writers to the state and society provoked an inner conflict in many European poets which deeply affected their work. The trouble began in the years after the First World War with disorder and disillusion and reached a crisis in the Wall Street crash of 1928 and the consequent spread of unemployment on an enormous scale throughout Europe. It is not surprising that at this time some poets, seeking to find a remedy for the ills of humanity, looked for a vast change on the Russian model and believed all too readily what the Russians told them. In Germany particularly a savage spirit was lurking just below the surface, and if many of its energies were later to be absorbed by the paranoiac barbarism of the Nazis, it was also responsible for something more interesting. Of it Bertolt Brecht (1898–1956) was a formidable exponent. He was by birth a man of the middle class, and his good education acquainted him with the literature of other languages than German. Yet almost from the start he nursed a destructive hatred for the society in which he lived. In the

First World War he became a medical orderly in a military hospital, and what he saw there left him with an incurable horror of war and all that it stands for. This found full utterance in his sour and splendid 'Legende vom toten Soldaten' ('Legend of the dead Soldier'),[16] which, in its revivification of a dead soldier by alcohol and his public parade through the streets, gives a horrifying image of the hypocrisy and callousness of war. Brecht was a war-casualty in the sense that war fixed him in a mould of bitter opposition which he never broke, and though at times he recalls our own soldiers' songs, he is moved by a characteristically German bitterness and operates not with humour but with wit. He was primarily a dramatist, but he was also an unusual kind of lyrical poet, brilliantly imaginative and capable of giving lurid shapes to many forms of hate and contempt. His talents were fully at work when in 1928 he produced his *Dreigroschenoper* (*Threepenny Opera*) which is an up-to-date, savage, and socially conscious adaptation of John Gay's *Beggar's Opera*. Thus the highwayman Macheath, who in Gay has a certain rude geniality, becomes a sinister figure of modern life, a moving spirit behind oppression and exploitation and murder, who is not himself punished for his crimes. Brecht's treatment of him can be seen from the first verses of a song with which the play opens and which gains enormously from the haunting, melancholy tune composed by Kurt Weill, but is none the less deeply disturbing in its own right:

> Und der Haifisch, der hat Zähne
> Und die trägt er im Gesicht
> Und Macheath, der hat ein Messer
> Doch das Messer sieht man nicht.
>
> Ach, es sind des Haifischs Flossen
> Rot, wenn dieser Blut vergiesst!
> Mackie Messer trägt 'nen Handschuh
> Drauf man keine Untat liest.[17]

> *And the shark has rows of teeth,*
> *And he shows them in his face,*
> *And Macheath, he has a knife,*
> *But that knife can no man trace.*

*Oh the shark's fins are scarlet*
*When upon them blood is spread,*
*But Knife Mackie wears a glove*
*Where his crimes cannot be read.*

This is sharp and angry against the oppressors of mankind. The simplicity of the form adds to its force, and though it is a powerful instrument of controversy and indoctrination, it is still authentic poetry. Yet this is not the only field in which Brecht reveals his powers. His hatred for certain sections of society was ultimately based on his compassion for their victims, and these were not confined to the poor and the underprivileged. Brecht is no less touched by those whom society has broken by more insidious means, by driving them to vice and other escapes from reality. It is of these that he speaks in 'Ballade von den Abenteuern' ('Ballad of the Adventurers'). Excluded alike from heaven and hell, they would have been better not to have been born, but even for them Brecht has a word as he tells of their disastrous lives and the dream which haunts them:

Schlendernd durch Höllen und gepeitscht durch Paradiese
Still und grinsend vergehenden Gesichts
Traümt er gelegentlich von einer kleinen Wiese
Mit blauen Himmel drüber und sonst nichts.[18]

*Strolling through Hells and lashed through Paradises,*
*In silence, with a smirking face half-dead,*
*From time to time he dreams of a small meadow,*
*With nothing but a blue sky overhead.*

In such moods, in which he is most himself, Brecht speaks from his full nature and is none the less a popular poet, for what he says was at the time deeply felt by a very large number of people and was in no sense esoteric or cryptic. The success of the *Threepenny Opera* was such that the Nazis punished even those who had gramophone-records of it, and Brecht's songs were as popular in Germany as the songs of musical comedies. At this time Brecht, like Mayakovsky in his best years, combined a truly poetical and personal utterance with a passionate concern for public affairs and an ability to translate it into moving and highly original poetry.

Yet, again like Mayakovsky, Brecht plainly felt that he was not doing enough, that his poetry must make a more immediate and more specific impact and create not merely a general mood but intellectual and moral attitudes for individual occasions and causes. That he should think this is understandable; for he felt very strongly about the issues which he advocated and wished to give every possible help to them. Yet he was wrong in underestimating the influence of his poetical gifts and in overestimating his ability to make propaganda by less exacting means. He never lost his lyrical genius, but he tended to dilute it and to cut out its more striking qualities. When Hitler came to power in 1933, Brecht wrote a cycle of songs on him to be sung to respected hymn-tunes,[19] and this bizarre experiment enforces the contrast between Hitler's professed aims and his actual behaviour. Brecht derides Hitler as a house-painter, who wishes to refurbish Germany but covers it with his filthy brown mess and leaves it worse than before. In all this there is undoubted power, but we miss the fullness of Brecht's daemonic impact. He has curbed his genius in order to drive his message home, and his message is poorer in consequence. Abstractions, however persuasive and ingenious, are inadequate substitutes for the spontaneous lyrical note, and Brecht is too prone to them and to the didactic spirit which goes with them. In this he is typical of a whole class of poets who shared his views and gave a special turn to the political poetry of the thirties.

In 1928 Brecht became a Marxist, and on the advent of Hitler to power left Germany. He was now completely committed to the class-struggle and gave all his gifts to it. In his dramatic work he showed an astonishing ingenuity and invention, and with it won his greatest successes, chiefly, it must be admitted, in non-Communist countries. But he continued to write verse, which was always well made and effective, but just as he simplified his manner for popular consumption, he also simplified his emotions and concentrated on those which he believed to be shared by a large number of sympathisers. Just as the Victorians tried to say the confessedly right thing about public events, so Brecht concentrated on single points which could be easily assimilated and involved no conflict or complexity. The results are by no means negligible. When most Germans pretended that they had never heard of concentration-camps, Brecht wrote about them and offered hope and consolation to their victims by telling them that they would be the true leaders of Germany through their undefeated defence of the truth.[20] This is impressive at first sight, but not quite convincing and not quite true. By putting so much emphasis on endurance Brecht seems almost to have forgotten the suffering which calls for it. He sees the victims of persecution from too simplified a point of view and gives a very inadequate notion of them. In his eagerness to drive home a single point he impoverishes his poetry, for it was not in this field that his finest gifts lay. Yet though Brecht made these sacrifices for the cause in which he believed, they were miscalculated. Neither in Moscow nor later in East Germany were his plays acted till after his death, and in this he again resembles Mayakovsky. He was much too independent and too critical for the authorities to be sure of him. And in his poetry what lasts and gains in popularity is precisely those pieces into which he has put the whole of his contradictory self and which rise from that sympathy for the human lot which lay beneath his harsh manner and his cruel jokes. Brecht was a true poet almost in spite of himself, and his attempts to force himself into a pattern fortunately did not absorb all his efforts.

The political turmoil of the thirties, with its bloated tyrannies and their menace to the whole civilised world, confronted poets with a hard decision. The art in which most of them had been brought up was not well equipped for dealing with large emotions and wide horizons, but they could not always escape from prevalent movements in politics or fail to take up a position with regard to them, and sometimes this had the urgency of religious conversion. Once they had embraced a cause there was nothing they would not dedicate to it, including their own precious and carefully nurtured art. If poets were expected to have a message, they were prepared to provide it. For some the change was especially difficult because they had been brought up in poetical techniques, such as Dadaism and Surrealism, which could hardly be expected to have any popular appeal and did not aim at clarity of expression. Yet they felt that they must get into closer touch with their fellow-men and find a sense of unity with them, and for this their art was ill-equipped. A poet may wish to sink his personality in that of others, whose sufferings he shares or would like to share, and to speak both for them and with them, in the simplicity of natural man faced by hideous dangers and driven back on his basic human state. His change of mood calls for a change of style, for a manner which will enable him to identify himself with others on issues which none can escape. But such an adjustment is never easy, and at times it may cost more than it is worth. The problem is to find a new manner which is as poetically effective as the old but which speaks for a wider range of experience to a larger audience. The challenge has been taken by some highly gifted poets, and in their responses we can see what is gained and what is lost.

The Spanish Civil War, which broke out in 1936, not only cost Spain a million dead but appealed to poets all over the world as a test of western civilisation in its most mature and humane form. Like Russia at the time of the Revolution, Spain at the outbreak of the Civil War could muster an array of poets which had no equal since the Golden Age. Most of them were on the side of the Republican government and wrote freely about their feelings for it and for the Spanish people. But their poetry was of a delicate kind which sought to state with precision and subtlety their own varied moods. It was admirably intimate, evocative, and melodious, but it was not well equipped for public affairs. So long as the poets wrote about their own experience in the Civil War, all was well; for they could use their advanced technique to give an exact form to their new experience. But some of them felt called to do more than this, to speak for their country in its agony, to appeal to large audiences and encourage their fellows in their heroic efforts. An example of what happened may be seen in Rafael Alberti (b. 1900). He was a bold experimentalist, who began with songs on traditional models and then evolved a highly intellectual Surrealism, in which he depicted with a stern integrity his own inner conflicts. He evidently decided that this manner was not suited to the Civil War, and tried to find simpler methods of dealing with it. His themes are now of the most obvious kind—besieged Madrid, General Kleber, the International Brigade, the death of Lorca, the familiar scenes of the battlefield. He has forsaken his brilliant use of free verse for more conventional forms, and his poetical personality has lost much of its rarity and richness. Yet Alberti remains a true poet. Though he is deeply committed to his cause, he does not debase his art for it; he fashions a new form of it which is suited to the simpler emotions with which he now deals. He does not write down to his audience but presents his own feelings as the war has simplified them. His verses were widely quoted, and if he wished to give practical help to his fellows, he certainly succeeded. The only doubt that may trouble us is that in his choice of themes he oversimplifies a complex situation and therefore fails to make the most of it. He comes to war as a novice and has to begin at the beginning, with perhaps less knowledge than many others. This simplicity is quite genuine, but it is not what we expect from Alberti, and to this degree his poems on the Civil War lack some of his most marked and most engaging characteristics. He is at his best when he relaxes this desire to make everything clear and allows himself a more generous indulgence in his usual imagery, and then, though he is certainly less complex than in his earlier work, he looks on the events of the Civil War with a momentary detachment and speaks of his own feelings because he must and not because it may help others. So in 'Monte de el Pardo' he describes the effect which the bright light of the battlefield makes on him and how it turns his mind to thoughts of death:

Todo esto me remuerde, me socava, me quita
ligereza a los ojos, me los nubla y me pone
la conciencia cargada de llanto y dinamita.
La soledad retumba y el sol se descompone.[21]

*All this gnaws me, and undermines me, takes*
*the lightness from my eyes, mists them, and lays*
*a load of tears and dynamite on my mind.*
*Loneliness echoes, and the sun decays.*

This is the authentic reflection of a poet who so absorbs his strange surroundings that he is able to present both them and himself from a new angle and to snatch a moment of illumination from the mechanised monotony of war.

Alberti is not a proletarian poet, either by origin, or by poetical training, or by actual achievement. He wished to speak for the Spanish people and did so in a reformed version of his earlier manner. He made far less sacrifices of his art than Mayakovsky or even Brecht, and perhaps part of his success lies in seeing that there is no such thing as a truly proletarian manner and that his task was to provide authentic poetry which would appeal to a large audience. His decision may be illustrated by the work of his friend Miguel Hernández (1910–42). He was indeed a man of the people, the son of a goatherd, but, encouraged by Machado and Jiménez, he had before the Civil War written poems in the elaborate manner of Góngora, who had a strong appeal for the successors of the Symbolists. When the war came, he fought in it, and eventually died in prison, after writing some remarkable poems to his wife and to the son whom he had never seen. He wrote of the war with a new gravity and ease and caught its exalting spirit. His verses were recited in the trenches of the Republican army and became popular in the fullest sense. Yet in them, though Hernández abandoned his first mannerisms, as he would anyhow have done, he makes no concessions to his audience. As a man of the people he knew his fellows from inside, and saw what their real taste was and how readily they would respond to authentic poetry, even if it made demands on them. He was fortunate also in that he was naturally a simple man and that his reactions were extremely direct and straightforward. This enabled him to write about war without effort or affectation and to speak about matters on which a more sophisticated poet would have had reservations. Thus he faces the possibility of death with a straightforward candour and says exactly what he thinks about it:

> Si me muero, que me muera,
> con la cabeza muy alta.
> Muerto y veinte veces muerto,
> la boca contra la grama,
> tendré apretados los dientes
> y decidida la barba.
>
> Cantando espero la muerte,
> que hay ruiseñores que cantan
> encima de los fusiles
> y en medio de las batallas.[22]

> *If I die, let me die,*
> *With my head held even higher.*
> *Dead and twenty times dead,*
> *my mouth against the couch-grass,*
> *I shall keep my teeth pressed together*
> *and my beard resolute.*
>
> *Singing I wait for death*
> *which has nightingales that sing*
> *above the rifles*
> *and in the middle of battles.*

This is simple but not simplified. Hernández speaks as a soldier to other soldiers, and they will understand him and take him at his full worth. The old form of the *romance* suits both his sentiments and his public, and he gives it an epic quality which it can well sustain.

The problems posed to Spanish poets were not unlike those posed to certain French poets by the fall of France and the German occupation. The Surrealists practised an intensely personal and often hermetic art, and before 1940 this caused them no trouble. But in 1940 and the succeeding years events were too strong for them, and they turned their highly trained words to speak of their country's fate. When a copy of *Le Crève-*

*cœur* (*Heart-break*), by Louis Aragon (b. 1897), was smuggled into England,[23] it made a powerful impression, if only because lovers of poetry were asking what the enormous catastrophe meant to France. It seemed then to speak for France in her agony, for Aragon was certainly appalled by what had happened, and tried as a poet to come to terms with it. These poems were all the more surprising because they were written by a man who had hitherto seemed to be rather finicky and sentimental and lacking in compulsive power. There is no doubt of the generous sweep of his emotions or of his ability to sketch the devastated scene and its heart-broken victims. In 'Les Lilas et les Roses' ('The Lilacs and the Roses')[24] he tells of the French countryside in all the glory of the spring and contrasts with it the misery and the confusion which defile it. His account is well observed, skilful, pathetic, and maintained in a single elegiac mood. In speaking of the sorrows of France Aragon seems to have fallen into a traditional temper, and yet we wonder whether after all such a mood is right for this stricken scene. We suspect that it is an escape from reality, an attempt to see an enormous chaos with the eyes of an older generation, which never knew anything like it and was likely to face it in a mood which lulls and comforts but does not really strike a central truth. Aragon has not responded with his whole being to what he sees, but presents instead what is ultimately a conventional view canonised by tradition and familiar to any reader. We can understand why he does this, but it means that his poetry has hardly survived the acid tests of time, if only because the events of which he speaks are more serious than his treatment suggests. No doubt he felt that this was the mood of the average Frenchman, and that he was right to assert it, but in retrospect we can see that he underrated the power of poetry to interpret human feelings and did not look deeply enough into his subject.

Another Surrealist, more gifted than Aragon, underwent a not dissimilar change under pressure from events. Paul Éluard (1895–1952) had hitherto written largely about love and its variations and was fully at home in evoking remote associations and subtle echoes, but he had also been interested in politics and developed for them a second, simpler manner. When under the German occupation the Resistance was beginning to count its martyrs, he strengthened this way of writing and fell into grave, measured tones, with nothing that calls for explanation or suggests dim vistas beyond itself. When he honours the death of a victim of the Germans, he uses regular lines and the most ordinary words in the plainest possible way:

> La nuit qui précéda sa mort
> Fut la plus courte de sa vie
> L'idée qu'il existait encore
> Lui brûlait la sang aux poignets
> Le poids de son corps l'écœurait
> Sa force le faisait gémir
> C'est tout au fond de cette horreur
> Qu'il a commencé à sourir
> Il n'avait pas UN camarade
> Mais des millions et des millions
> Pour le venger il le savait
> Et le jour se leva pour lui[25]

> *The night that came before his death*
> *Was the shortest in all his life.*
> *The thought that he was still alive*
> *Set the blood burning to his wrists,*
> *His body's weight disgusted him,*
> *His strength forced a groan out of him.*
> *It was right at this horror's start*
> *That he began to show a smile.*
> *He had not ONE companion,*
> *But millions and millions*
> *To work his vengeance—that he knew,—*
> *And so the dawn arose for him.*

Éluard's stern restraint is more moving and more satisfying than Aragon's plangent grief, and his short sentences lead to a noble climax in the death of a man who feels that all France is with him, while the dawn which rises as he dies is an apt symbol of what his death means. In this piece, as in others of the time, Éluard has reacted against the subtleties of private experience and tried to find an alternative suited to a heroic occasion. For his own art it means not merely a thorough simplification but a stricter sense of order, since many of his previous poems look more like materials for poetry than poetry itself. Though he concedes quite as much as Mayakovsky or Brecht to public needs and adapts his style quite as thoroughly, he is less abstract and intrudes no hint of doctrine. Yet this called for an effort, and Éluard illustrates what it costs a poet to change his direction once he has found it. He manages to do so for a while because external forces compel him, and the results are by any standards impressive. But he has not put all his gifts, and certainly not his most unusual gifts, into this manner, and in the end he is the victim of an unresolved conflict between his lifelong attachment to his own inner world and his consciousness of obligations to his fellow-men. He illustrates a predicament in our time. Poets like him have begun by assimilating the highly self-conscious art of an individualistic society and then found themselves trapped in public events. They have courageously tried to adapt themselves and have to some measure succeeded, but this has prevented a complete fulfilment of themselves or their integration into a complete poetical personality. They were born too early to turn their private outlooks to public themes without paying a heavy price, and their high degree of sophistication has hampered their complete identification of themselves with their new subjects. Thus in spite of all their care and sincerity a touch of aridity has crept into their otherwise ebullient creations.

It is not easy for poets to adjust either their natural gifts or their training to entirely strange conditions, but in these cases it was helped by the extreme urgency and unescapable pressure of political needs. Poets found themselves flung into them and improvised brilliantly to meet their call. The hideous present could not be shirked or forgotten, and so dark was it that only through some triumph of poetry could the poet defeat it in himself. In Germany, Spain, and France the situation called for action, no matter how secret or subterranean, and the poet could at least contribute his quota of help in words. In Great Britain there was no crisis comparable to what was happening elsewhere, and the opiates so skilfully administered by Baldwin in his years of power might seem to have lulled the British public into a complacent indifference to the fate of the world. But it was just this much advertised security which stung a young generation of poets into protest and complaint. They were in the first place moved by the social condition of their own country, where a dismal acceptance of an outmoded system seemed to offer no hope to a large part of the population. In this they were the heirs of a long tradition of British radicalism, which goes back to William Morris and Shelley and Milton. But in the second place the standards by which they judged their own country and found it wanting were equally relevant abroad, where in the rise of the Nazis, the slaughter of the Viennese socialists by Dollfuss in 1934, the invasion of China by Japan, and the Spanish Civil War deadly threats were manifest to the structure of free societies and the essential prerequisites of a civilised life. Their powerful reactions to these new horrors came not from any fear for their own safety but from their outraged consciences and their innate sense of human worth. They were driven not by personal danger, as Brecht and Éluard were, but by abstract beliefs which meant a great deal to them. It is true that in their denunciations of Hitler and Franco they said nothing about Stalin, who had already begun to follow his murderous manias, but that was largely because they thought in abstractions and innocently regarded Communism as vastly superior to the new tyrannies and not at all like them. They suffered from not being immediately engaged in the events of which they wrote, and perhaps for this very reason they felt that they must speak in a more public and more simple way than was habitual to them.

These poets operated as a group, and though their individual gifts were remarkably diverse, their approach to public affairs was shared by all. The effort to adapt themselves to the common man and to speak a common language was not easy for any of them, and those who attempted least probably achieved most. Louis MacNeice (1907–63) was able without much effort to incorporate personal considerations of politics into his neat, carefully controlled art and felt no need to extend his already conversational manner to more proletarian uses. He remained very much himself, but shrank from handling large issues in their far-ranging character. Stephen Spender (b. 1909) liked large issues and spoke of them as a serious moralist in his own grave tones, but in dealing with Starhemberg or Franco felt himself so close to their victims that he relaxed and debased his speech and lost some of his characteristic dignity. Cecil Day Lewis (b. 1904) is naturally a lyrical poet of much delicacy and sensibility, and, though he always maintains his fine, selective language, his emotions turn a little harsh when he thinks about political horrors, and his violence rings a bit out of tune. W. H. Auden (b. 1907) began with the great advantage of being able to fall into the moods of other men and to shape events into dramatic patterns. Add to these gifts his strong, if sometimes whimsical, moral feelings, and he would seem to have the right qualifications for a political poet in times of crisis. In the thirties he had a keen eye for the greatness and the baseness of the human race and wrote about it with a bold fluency and many moments of power and insight. But just because he was not personally involved in events, he lacks the immediacy which we find in the opponents of the Nazis or in the Spanish Republicans or in the members of the French Resistance. Poetry of this kind lives on bitter, personal experience, and without it it almost inevitably falls into abstract morality which does not quite touch the heart.

If the call of politics is responsible for rifts in the art of Mayakovsky, Brecht, Éluard and other 'committed' poets, it was at least answered by deliberate choice, and, for better or for worse, they are themselves responsible for their decisions. But the rift which conditions produced in them may be natural to a man and part of his inborn equipment for poetry. This is the case with the remarkable Chilean poet, Pablo Neruda (b. 1904), who is still busily at work. He was from the start a man of the people. His father was a railway employee, and he himself knew what it is to be poor in a country which has more than its fair share of poverty. But, as such men will, Neruda managed to get himself educated and had written five volumes of verse before he was twenty-one. His efforts were rewarded by a series of government posts, which enabled him to come to Europe and meet the chief Spanish poets before the Civil War. Since 1943 he has been a member of the Communist party, and though this meant that in 1949 he had to retire to exile in Mexico, in 1953 he returned to Chile, where he lives more or less undisturbed. The Chilean treatment of Neruda contrasts favourably with the Russian treatment of Mayakovsky and Pasternak. He has been vociferously in opposition for many years, but he has been able to write and to publish.

Neruda's production is enormous, and one half of it is very poor stuff indeed, political rhetoric unredeemed by imagination or insight. But the other half is by any standards remarkable, and the division between the bad and the good is not so much within single poems as between one poem and another, as if Neruda had good and bad days for writing. The extremely uneven character of his work might be ascribed to his determination not to be guided by conventional notions of good taste. He has said firmly: 'Those who shun the "bad taste" of things will fall on their face in the snow',[26] but this is not relevant to his own performance as an artist; he means that we must look on the ugly side of things as well as on the beautiful. Neruda does not flout current standards for the pleasure of it; he is practically unaware of them. When he writes, he usually has something to say, and the way in which he says it depends entirely on the quality of his mood at the moment. Neruda puts his whole nature and experience into his poetry, and much of this is unredeemably prosaic. But at his best, and his best is remarkably abundant, he is an astonishing poet, with an impetus not paralleled in this century and an ability to convey all kinds of mood in their untrammelled richness. Though he has been much in Europe and though in his youth he read the French and Spanish poets then in vogue, he seems to owe very little to them. His strength comes from his Latin-American origin, his humble birth, his early life among simple people, his roots in a country where modernity lies very lightly on ancient foundations.

The primitive element in Neruda is largely responsible for his imagery, which is sometimes crude and violent, often unusually apt, and nearly always original. He thinks in images as primitive people do, and even when he draws on modern phenomena for them, he is entirely their master. They are his natural means of utterance, and when he fails, it is usually because he resorts instead to dull, abstract words and standardised ideas. This is the other side of his character, which has been imposed on his essential self by political textbooks and is totally uninteresting. As a man of the people Neruda wishes to be understood by them. He would like his poems to be 'useful and usable like metal and corn'; he calls on simplicity to teach him 'how to sing a floodtide of virtue and truth'; he longs to be one with his people and claims that he writes 'with your life and my own'.[27] This is the creed of a man who has never felt the lure of solitude or sought to fashion a private universe of the imagination. So when he deals with political matters, he feels that he is speaking for multitudes and has all their weight and support behind him. In his bad work, this makes him worse as he deals out his platitudes, but in his good work it sharpens his attack, as if he were defending a cause with all his powers and straining everything to make it succeed. A simple example is 'La United Fruit Co.', written about American exploitation of the 'Banana Republics' of Central America. He begins by denouncing the Company which has created its own *opéra bouffe* and is responsible for the various tyrants who dominate the Caribbean and whom he compares with flies 'buzzing drunkenly on the populous middens'. But behind the fierce bravado of his attack lies his essential humanity, his compassion for the unregarded victims of a merciless system, for his own Latin-Americans who are mere instruments for the production of coffee and fruit:

Mientras tanto, por los abismos
azucarados de los puertos,
caían indios sepultados
en el vapor de la mañana:
un cuerpo rueda, una cosa
sin nombre, un número caído,
un racimo de fruta muerta
derramada en el pudridero.[28]

*All the while, in the sugary*
*abysses of the seaports,*
*Indians fall, ensepulchred*
*in the vapour of the morning:*
*a body swirls away, a thing*
*without name, a fallen number,*
*a branch of dead fruit*
*spilled in the carrion-vat.*

Neruda has many moments of such humanity, and they are entirely instinctive and natural. Other Communist poets may feel that it is their duty to champion the oppressed, but Neruda does it because he feels that he belongs to them and shares their sorrows.

Neruda's bad poetry is often full of Marxist doctrine stated with a rhetorical emphasis which does not add to its attraction. This might persuade us that Marxism as such is hostile to poetry and cannot be assimilated into it, and this is true if we mean Marxist doctrine with all the emphasis on doctrine. But it is equally true of imperialism as it was preached eighty years ago or of Catholicism as we see it in large tracts of Péguy and Claudel. It is not the aim or the bias of a doctrine that resists truly poetical treatment but the mere fact that it is a doctrine, abstract thought in abstract terms, and so shaped to suit large numbers of people that it deals only with conventional sentiments and lacks any life of its own. Doctrines strongly held can of course inspire noble poetry, but only by shedding their doctrinal stiffness and allowing free play to their treatment. This is particularly relevant to the present world in which much doctrine is more carefully formulated and more rigid than ever before, while poetry aims at an increasingly personal idiosyncrasy. The gap between doctrine and poetry is too great for even the best poets to bridge with any success, and though their efforts may not be disastrous, they fall below their right level of achievement. Attempts to create a wider public for poetry by dispensing instruction and indoctrination fail because the poetry itself is lost in the process. The hope that an age of vast social changes might create a truly popular poetry has been frustrated largely by attempts to provide sermons and pamphlets in verse instead of following the true creative instinct which by its very nature refuses to submit to conformity, whether in thought or in feeling.

The attempt of poets to reach a wider public through simplifying their art is based on more than one misconception. The idea, prevalent in Russia, that most poetry was bourgeois and must be replaced by the true proletarian article was contradicted by their own practice. But it might still have some truth in it. In fact in most countries it has very little indeed. Where proletarian poetry exists, it is usually a survival from an old folk-art and has few possibilities of development, and truly proletarian poets like Hernández and Neruda have no difficulty in expressing themselves in an established idiom which is called bourgeois. The notion of bourgeois poetry is too foggy to be of any value, and in Communist countries the adjective is applied to any art which the authorities may at the moment dislike. But there remains a real problem. The literature of a country should speak for it in all possible aspects and appeal to as large as possible a portion of its inhabitants. This was the case in ancient Greece, and it is still the case in some countries where distinctions of wealth have not created fundamental distinctions of culture. For instance, in Somaliland Maḥammed 'Abdille Ḥasan, who was known to the British as 'the Mad Mullah' and led his Dervishes in many attacks on British outposts before his death in 1920, was a considerable poet, who wrote in the classical manner of his countrymen on contemporary and highly provocative subjects and showed a talent for derision, abuse, and scorn, which greatly delighted his followers.[29] His main themes were drawn from his struggle with the British, and his poems, though written in a literary language, were known throughout his country. When Mao Tse-tung or Ho Chi-minh writes poetry about current events, it may be in a traditional style but it is known to millions of people. Even in some European countries, notably Russia and Spain, workers on the land or in factories have often shown that they are capable of liking a much more elaborate poetry than their rulers or even their writers expect, and if this poetry concerns public affairs, they welcome it all the more readily, since it also concerns them. Difficulty arises only in a country where social and educational distinctions are such that different classes read different kinds of books, and some may read none at all. If this is still partly the case in England, it is because our educational system is not yet universal. But when it becomes so, we should expect those who like poetry at all to like it whatever their social background may be. There is no case for one poetry for the rich and another for the poor. At the moment poetry is not read so much as it has been in the past, and though there are many reasons for this, one is that it is introvert and specialised and lacks the impulse to attack large issues. But this state of affairs need not last for ever and may even be an interval of preparation in which poets forge new weapons before taking larger risks and regaining some of the territory which they have lost from being too particular about their aims.

Poetry on public events has as much right to exist as poetry on any other subject, since it helps us to grasp them from unexpected angles and to treat them seriously without yielding to the numbing influence of lower methods of communication. Nor is there any reason why it should not be as good as other poetry in other fields. Poetry is concerned with our whole sentient being, and we must be less or more than human if we are indifferent to what happens around us and is likely sooner or later to strike us at some vital point. All that matters is that it should do its own work and not that of some other less exalted medium. In our own century political poetry has been restricted by two formidable obstacles, the persistence of public utterance from the nineteenth century and the unwillingness of modern poets to venture into fields outside their daily purview. The first has been completely overcome, and though the second has been breached with brilliant success at a few points, it has not been entirely reduced. Poetry moves forward by exploiting each new position to its limit and then abandoning it. It may yet decide that public affairs are not so alien and recalcitrant as it now tends to think, and pay more attention to them. If it does, we may be rewarded by a fuller, more eager, and more sensitive consciousness of what happens in the world to which we belong.

# NOTES

## CHAPTER I

1  *Inferno*, III, 59–60.
2  *Ibid.* XIX, 52–7.
3  At least not in his published text, but in an earlier draft Tennyson is said to have written 'Nolan had blunder'd'. Nolan had in fact sounded the bugle-call for the charge.
4  On the notion of 'Holy Russia' see Michael Cherniavsky, *Tsar and People* (Yale University Press, 1961), pp. 101–27.
5  F. Tyutchev, *Polnoye Sobraniye Stikhotvorenii* (Sovetskii Pisatel', Leningrad, 1957), p. 201.

> Эти бедные селенья,
> Эта скудная природа —
> Край родной долготерпенья,
> Край ты русского народа!
>
> Не поймет и не заметит
> Гордый взор иноплеменный,
> Что сквозит и тайно светит
> В наготе твоей смиренной.
>
> Удрученный ношей крестной,
> Всю тебя, земля родная,
> В рабском виде царь небесный
> Исходил, благословляя.

> *These poor hamlets, humbly faring,*
> *Nature sunk in desolation,*
> *Land of mine such sorrows bearing,*
> *Land of all the Russian nation!*
>
> *Nothing knowing, nothing seeing,*
> *How can haughty foreign faces*
> *Mark what mystery has being*
> *In thy lowly, naked places?*
>
> *There was one, my land, who knew thee:*
> *With a cross upon him pressing,*
> *Like a servant walking through thee,*
> *Heaven's king bestowed his blessing.*

6  G. Carducci, *Poesie* (Zanichelli, Bologna, 1937), pp. 884–7. Carducci reaches his climax in the sixteenth and seventeenth stanzas·

Tra boschi immani d'agavi non mai
mobili ad aura di benigno vento,
sta ne la sua piramide, vampante
livide fiamme

per la tenèbra tropicale, il dio
Huitzilopotli, che il tuo sangue fiuta,
e navigando il pelago co 'l guardo
ulula — Vieni.

*Through the vast forests of agaves, no longer
Stirring to the motion of friendly breezes,
Rising up from his pyramid and breathing
Blasts of a black flame,*

*He, the god, thro' dusk of the tropic twilight,
Huitzilopotli, for your blood is thirsting;
With his eyes he searches the open waters,
Murmurs: 'Come hither!'*

With Carducci's romantic and historical treatment of the theme we
may compare Manet's picture, painted in 1867 and now at Mainz, of
the shooting of Maximilian. Manet paints the scene with dispassionate
realism and conveys through the gestures of the firing squad their
purely professional interest in the execution.

7  *Poems of Gerard Manley Hopkins*, 3rd ed. (Oxford University Press, 1948),
p. 107, and *The Letters of Gerard Manley Hopkins to Robert Bridges*, ed.
C. C. Abbott, rev. ed. (Oxford University Press, 1955), p. 274.

8  *Poems of Gerard Manley Hopkins*, p. 168. The last of the four stanzas
illustrates the fatuity and falseness of the whole poem:

Where is the field I must play the man on?
O welcome there their steel or cannon.
Immortal beauty is death with duty,
If under her banner I fall for her honour.
(Ch.) Under her banner we fall for her honour.

9  It is characteristic of him that, when he wrote 'Recessional' after
Queen Victoria's Diamond Jubilee in 1897, he threw it into the waste-
paper basket, no doubt feeling that its authentic emotions were un-
suited to a time of imperial celebration. Fortunately it was salvaged by
Miss Sarah Norton and published in *The Times* (see C. Carrington,
*Rudyard Kipling*, Macmillan, London, 1955, p. 264).

10  Thomas Hardy, *Collected Poems* (Macmillan and Co., London, 1951),
p. 350.

11  A. Rimbaud, *Œuvres complètes*, édition Pléiade (Paris, 1946), p. 64.

12  *Ibid.* p. 66.

13  Thomas Hardy, *Collected Poems*, p. 559.
14  Siegfried Sassoon, *Collected Poems* (Faber and Faber, London, 1947), p. 124.
15  Valery Bryusov, *Puti y Pereput'ya* (Skorpion, Moscow, 1908), p. 212. The notion of Russia as 'the Third Rome' appears in a letter from the monk Philotheos to Grand Prince Vasily III of Moscow, early in the sixteenth century: 'And now there is the Holy Synodal Apostolic church of the third reigning Rome, of your tsardom, which shines like the sun in its orthodox Christian faith throughout the whole universe', quoted by Cherniavsky, *Tsar and People*, p. 38.
16  On the subject in general see Oleg A. Maslenikov, *The Frenzied Poet* (University of California Press, 1952), which deals mainly with Bely and Blok, but gives also a good account of Soloviev.
17  A. Blok, *Polnoye Sobraniye Stikhotvorenii*, 1 (Sovetskii Pisatel', Moscow, 1946), pp. 501–5.
18  *Ibid.* p. 508. Note especially the second stanza:

> Лодки, да гради по рекам рубила ты,
> Но до Царьградских святынь не дошла...
> Соколов, лебедей в степь распустила ты—
> Кинулась из степи черная мгла...
>
> *Boats, yes, and towns on your rivers they hew for you,*
> *But you came not to the Emperor's Town...*
> *Hawks and wild swans on the steppe rose and flew for you—*
> *Over the steppe a black mist settles down.*

19  N. Gumilev, *Koster* (Grzhebin, Petersburg–Berlin, 1922), p. 23.
20  O. Mandel'shtam, *Stikhotvoreniya* (Gosudarstvennoye Izdatel'stvo, Moscow–Leningrad, 1928), p. 23.
21  Anna Akhmatova, *Anno Domini* (Alkonost, Petersburg, 1923), p. 77:

> Ты всегда таинственный и новый,
> Я тебя послушней с каждым днем.
> Но любовь твоя, о друг суровый,
> Испытание железом и огнем.
>
> Запрещаешь петь и улыбаться,
> А молиться запретил давно.
> Только б мне с тобою не расстаться,
> Остальное все равно!
>
> Так, земле и небесам чужая,
> Я живу и больше не пою.
> Словно ты у ада и у рая
> Отнял душу вольную мою.

*You are always new and always hidden;*
*More each day I yield to your desire.*
*But your love, hard-hearted friend, has bidden*
*Me to tests of iron and of fire.*

*You forbid my song, forbid my laughter,*
*Long ago you told me not to pray.*
*But I care not for what happens after*
*If from you I am not cast away.*

*From the earth and skies you would me sever;*
*I live, and my songs have ceased to swell.*
*'Tis as if to my free soul for ever*
*You had shut both Paradise and Hell.*

22  *Anno Domini*, p. 90.
23  *Ibid.* p. 32. Translated in C. M. Bowra, *A Book of Russian Verse* (Macmillan, London, 1943), p. 117.
24  *Ibid.* p. 31. Translated Bowra, *op. cit.* p. 116.
25  Anna Akhmatova, *Izbrannye Stikhotvoreniya* (Chekov, New York, 1952), p. 222.
26  V. V. Mayakovsky, *Polnoye Sobraniye Sochinenii*, I (Gosudarstvennoye Izdatel'stvo, Moscow, 1939), p. 40. Translated by George Reavey in *The Bedbug and Selected Poetry* by Vladimir Mayakovsky (Weidenfeld and Nicolson, London, 1961), p. 53.
27  Georg Trakl, *Die Dichtungen* (Otto Müller, Salzburg, 1938), p. 37.
28  Ezra Pound, *Selected Poems* (Faber and Faber, London, 1947), p. 124.
29  J. M. Synge, *Collected Works*, I (Oxford University Press, 1962), p. xxxvi.

## CHAPTER 2

1  V. Ivanov, *Prozrachnost* (Skorpion, Moscow, 1908), p. 91.
2  Valery Bryusov, *Puti i Pereput'ya*, II (Skorpion, Moscow, 1908), p. 216. See D. Maksimov, *Poeziya Valeriya Bryusova* (Leningrad, 1940), pp. 188–9.
3  *The Genealogy of Morals*, I. 11.
4  *Thus Spake Zarathustra*, III. 12. 39.
5  Stefan George, *Werke*, I (Georg Bondi, München, 1958), p. 361:

> Zehntausend muss der heilige wahnsinn schlagen,
> Zehntausend muss die heilige seuche raffen,
> Zehntausende der heilige krieg.

> *Ten thousand must the holy madness strike,*
> *Ten thousand must the holy sickness seize,*
> *Tens of thousands the holy war.*

6 *Ibid.* pp. 435–41, the short play 'Der Brand des Tempels' shows how a ruthless conqueror sets out to destroy an ancient temple, which is the symbol of a tired civilisation, and there is no doubt that he is expected to win our approval.

7 Georg Trakl, *Die Dichtungen* (Otto Müller, Salzburg, 1938), p. 183.

8 *Ibid.* p. 197, especially

O stolzere Trauer! ihr ehernen Altäre,
Die heisse Flamme des Geistes nährt heute ein gewaltiger Schmerz,
Die ungebornen Enkel.

*O prouder sorrow! you altars of bronze,*
*The hot flame of the spirit is fed today by a powerful pain,*
*The unborn grandchildren.*

9 Georg Heym, *Dichtungen und Schriften*, I (Heinrich Ellermann, München, 1964), p. 440.

10 C. Cavafy, *Poiemata* (Alexandria, 1935), pp. 22–3. See G. Mikhaletos, *Kavafika Themata* (Athens, 1955), pp. 6–23.

11 V. V. Khlebnikov, *Izbrannye Stikhotvoreniya* (Sovetskii Pisatel', Moscow, 1936), p. 395.

12 Isaac Rosenberg, *Collected Poems* (Chatto and Windus, London, 1949), p. 89.

13 *The Letters of W. B. Yeats* (Rupert Hart-Davis, London, 1954), pp. 874–5.

14 A. Blok, *Polnoye Sobraniye Stikhotvorenii* (Sovetskii Pisatel', Moscow, 1946), p. 582.

15 Sophie Bonneau, *L' Univers poétique d'Alexandre Blok* (Paris, 1946), p. 192, quoting Blok's journal for 10 March 1918 where he begins by saying: 'If there existed a true clergy in Russia, it would long ago have taken notice of this fact, that Christ is with the Red Guards. The truth cannot be discussed. Have I glorified it? I have only established a fact.'

16 N. Gumilev, *Ognenii Stolp* (Petersburg–Berlin, 1922), p. 11, translated by Y. Hornstein.

17 A. Bely, *Stikhotvoreniya* (Grzhebin, Petersburg–Berlin, 1923), p. 463. See M. Cherniavsky, *Tsar and People*, pp. 224–5, and Bowra, *A Second Book of Russian Verse*, pp. 224–5.

18 V. V. Khlebnikov, *op. cit.* p. 407.

19 *Ibid.* p. 221.

20 V. Mayakovsky, *Sobraniye Stikhotvorenii* (Sovetskii Pisatel', Moscow, 1950), I, 271–324.

21 *Ibid.* I, 195–270.

22 *Ibid.* II, 53.

23 W. B. Yeats, *Collected Poems* (Macmillan and Co., London, 1950), pp. 210–11. J. Stallworthy, *Between the Lines* (Oxford University Press, 1963), pp. 16–25 gives an illuminating account of its origins and composition.

24 W. B. Yeats, *op. cit.* p. 263.

25 *Ibid.* p. 397. See Stallworthy, *op. cit.* pp. 222–42.

26 David Gascoyne, *Collected Poems* (Oxford University Press, 1965), p. 45. In the last section, called 'Ecce Homo', the contemporary nature of the theme is fully disclosed:

> See, the centurions wear riding-boots,
> Black shirts and badges and peaked caps,
> Greet one another with raised-arm salutes;
> They have cold eyes, unsmiling lips;
> Yet these His brothers know not what they do.
>
> And on either side hang dead
> A labourer and a factory-hand,
> And one is maybe a lynched Jew
> And one a Negro or a Red,
> Coolie or Ethiopian, Irishman,
> Spaniard or German democrat.

27 León Felipe, quoted by José Luis Cano, *El tema de España* (Revista de Occidente, Madrid, 1964), p. 24.

28 Luis Cernuda, *La realidad y el deseo* (Árbol, Mexico), pp. 183–4.

29 See José Luis Cano, *El tema de España*, pp. 24–30.

30 *Elegy for Spain* (Contemporary Bookshop, Manchester, 1939), p. 6.

31 *The Collected Poems of Edith Sitwell* (Macmillan and Co., London, 1957), p. 276.

32 *Ibid.* p. 370.

But the Cold is the highest mathematical Idea...the Cold is Zero—
The Nothing from which arose
All Being and all variation...It is the sound too high for our hearing, the
Point that flows

Till it becomes the line of Time...an endless positing
Of Nothing, or the Ideal that tries to burgeon
Into Reality through multiplying...Then Time froze

To immobility and changed to Space.

33 First printed in *Twentieth-Century German Verse*, ed. Patrick Bridgwater (Penguin Books, 1963), p. 307.

## CHAPTER 3

1  T. S. Eliot, *Collected Poems, 1909–1962* (Faber and Faber, London, 1963), p. 140.
2  *Ibid*, pp. 229–30.
3  This was not always true of Machado, who in November 1914 wrote 'España en Paz', *Obras* (Seneca, Mexico, 1940), p. 260, about the benefits which Spain enjoyed from neutrality, and denouncing the horrors of war. It is not a very successful venture, and we can understand that Machado did not wish to repeat it.
4  Antonio Machado, *Obras*, p. 859.
5  Quoted in full by José Luis Cano, *El tema de España*, pp. 187–90.
6  Giuseppe Ungaretti, *L'Allegria* (Preda, Milan, 1931), p. 17.
7  *Collected Poems of Sidney Keyes* (Routledge, London, 1945), pp. 111–12.
8  Patrick Bridgwater, *Twentieth-Century German Verse* (Penguin Books, London, 1963), p. 204.
9  C. Cavafy, *Poiemata* (Alexandria, 1936), p. 127.
10  After his defeat by the Romans under C. Caecilius Metellus, Kritolaos ran away and was thought to have been drowned; Diaios, who was defeated soon afterwards by L. Mummius Achaicus at Leukopetra, fled to his home at Megalopolis, where he killed his wife, burned his house, and himself took poison. The sack of Corinth by Mummius, as of Smyrna by Mustafa Kemal in 1922, followed soon after the defeat.
11  Mao Tse-tung, *Nineteen Poems* (Foreign Languages Press, Peking, 1958), p. 30.
12  Salvatore Quasimodo, *Giorno dopo Giorno* (Mondadori, Milan, 1947), p. 41.
13  The story of Pasternak and the Nobel Prize is admirably told by Robert Conquest, *Courage of Genius* (Collins and Harvill Press, London, 1961).
14  Boris Pasternak, *Sochineniya*, III (University of Michigan Press, 1961), pp. 63–4.
15  *Ibid.* p. 67.
16  *Ibid.* pp. 102 ff.
17  *Ibid.* p. 107.
18  G. Seferis, *Poiemata*, 5th ed. (Ikaros, Athens, 1964), p. 196; translated by Rex Warner (The Bodley Head, London, 1960), p. 78.
19  Dylan Thomas, *Collected Poems, 1934–1952* (Dent, London, 1952), p. 62.
20  Quoted by Patrick Bridgwater, *Twentieth-Century German Verse*, pp. 255–6.
21  H. B. Steiner, *Unruhe ohne Uhr* (Schneider, Heidelberg, 1954), p. 31.

22  Peter H. Lee, *Anthology of Korean Poetry* (John Day, New York, 1964), p. 166.
23  G. Seferis, *Poiemata*, p. 178, translated by Rex Warner, pp. 68–9.
24  Werner Bergengruen, *Figur und Schatten* (Die Arche, Zürich, 1958), p. 141.
25  Quasimodo, *op. cit.* p. 60.


CHAPTER 4

1  Dudley Fitts, *Anthology of Contemporary Latin-American Poetry* (New Directions, Norfolk, Conn., 1947), p. 264.
2  *Ibid.* p. 270.
3  *Ibid.* p. 268.
4  Sergei Esenin, *Stikhotvoreniya* (Gozlitizdat, Moscow, 1955), I, p. 321.
5  See Francisca de Graaf, *Serge Esénine* (E. J. Brill, Leyden, 1938), pp. 181 ff.
6  V. V. Khlebnikov, *Izbrannye Stikhotvoreniya* (Sovetskii Pisatel', Moscow, 1936), p. 472.
7  V. Mayakovsky, *Sobraniye Stikhotvorenii* (Sovetskii Pisatel', Leningrad, 1950), II, 462–6, translated by George Reavey in *The Bed-bug and Selected Poetry*, pp. 209–19.
8  *Literaturnaya Gazeta*, 9 and 20 December 1935.
9  Boris Pasternak, *An Essay in Autobiography* (Collins and Harvill Press, London, 1959), p. 103.
10  Mayakovsky, *op. cit.* p. 580.
11  The various versions are given in V. Mayakovsky, *Polnoye Sobraniye Sochinenii*, X (Gosudarstvennoe Izdatel'stvo, Moscow, 1941), pp. 185–90. See also V. Katanyan, *Mayakovsky* (Sovetskii Pisatel', Moscow, 1945), pp. 241–2, and Edward J. Brown in *Literature and Revolution in Soviet Russia, 1917–1962*, ed. Max Hayward and Leopold Labedz (Oxford University Press, 1963), pp. 48–50.
12  S. Yesenin-Volpin, *A Leaf of Spring* (Frederick A. Praeger, New York, 1961), p. 78.
13  *Ibid.* p. 7.
14  Interview by K. S. Karol in *L'Express*, 24 May 1962.
15  Quoted by Pierre Forgues in *Literature and Revolution*, p. 184.
16  Bertolt Brecht, *Gedichte und Lieder* (Suhrkamp, Frankfurt-am-Main, 1962), pp. 121–4. The poem was so disliked by German nationalists that because of it Brecht's name was fifth on the list of people to be arrested at the time of Hitler's first *Putsch* in 1923; Martin Esslin, *Brecht: a Choice of Evils* (Eyre and Spottiswoode, London, 1959), p. 55.
17  Brecht, *Gedichte und Lieder*, p. 79.

18 *Ibid.* p. 65.

19 Bertolt Brecht, *Gedichte 3* (Suhrkamp, Frankfurt-am-Main, 1961). Among the tunes are 'Nun danket alle Gott', 'Befiel du deine Wege', 'Ein feste Burg ist unser Gott' and 'Ein strenger Herr ist unser Gott'.

20 *Ibid.* pp. 54–5. The last lines are worth quoting both for their manner and their matter:

> Also seid ihr
> Verschwunden, aber
> Nicht vergessen
> Niedergeknüppelt, aber
> Nicht widerlegt
> Zusammen mit den allen unverbesserbar Weiterkämpfenden
> Unbelehrbar auf der Wahrheit Beharrenden
> Weiterhin die wahren
> Führer Deutschlands.

> *So you are*
> *Vanished, but*
> *Not forgotten*
> *Beaten down, but*
> *Not refuted*
> *Together with all who incorrigibly fight on*
> *Obstinately standing on the truth*
> *Henceforth the true*
> *Leaders of Germany.*

21 Rafael Alberti, *Poesía (1924–1944)* (Losada, Buenos Aires, 1946), p. 236.

22 Miguel Hernández, *Obras Completas* (Losada, Buenos Aires, 1960), p. 272.

23 *Le Crève-cœur* was published in 1942 by Horizon and La France Libre in London, with prefaces by André Labarthe and Cyril Connolly.

24 *Le Crève-cœur*, pp. 25–6.

25 Paul Éluard, *Au Rendez-vous Allemand* (Les Éditions de Minuit, Paris, 1946), p. 9.

26 Quoted by Ben Belitt in *Selected Poems of Pablo Neruda* (Grove Press, New York, 1961), p. 40.

27 *Ibid.* p. 24.

28 Pablo Neruda, *Canto General* (Losada, Buenos Aires, 1955), I, p. 163.

29 B. W. Andrzejewski and I. M. Lewis, *Somali Poetry* (Clarendon Press, 1964), pp. 66–103. Note in particular the poem on the death of Richard Corfield in the battle of Dul Madoba on 9 August 1913. Corfield disregarded his orders and went into action, where he was killed by a

Dervish bullet in the head. Maḥammed 'Abdille Ḥasan tells him what to say when 'Hell-destined' he sets out for the other world:

Say: 'Friend', I called, 'have compassion and spare me!'
Say: 'As I looked fearfully from side to side my heart
was plucked from its sheath.'
Say: 'My eyes stiffened as I watched with horror:
The mercy I implored was not granted.'

The story has lost nothing in the telling.

# INDEX